I0136919

F. W Chesson

The Dutch Republics of South Africa

F. W Chesson

The Dutch Republics of South Africa

ISBN/EAN: 9783744718745

Printed in Europe, USA, Canada, Australia, Japan

Cover: Foto ©ninafisch / pixelio.de

More available books at **www.hansebooks.com**

THE DUTCH REPUBLICS
OF SOUTH AFRICA;

Three Letters

TO

R. N. FOWLER, ESQ., M.P., AND CHARLES BUXTON, ESQ., M.P.,

BY

F. W. CHESSON.

"It would not do to agree that negroes are men, lest it should appear that whites are not."—MONTESQUIEU.

London:

PUBLISHED BY WILLIAM TWEEDIE, 337, STRAND.

Price Two Shillings.

1871.

LONDON:
GILBERT AND RIVINGTON, PRINTERS,
52, ST. JOHN'S SQUARE.

PREFACE.

THE first of the following Letters was published, although in a more extended form, at the close of the year 1868. It is now revised and reprinted, and two other Letters are added, in the hope that they will assist to form a public opinion favourable to the just treatment of the native races of South Africa. Every day the slave-trade is permitted to exist in that region the difficulty of its abolition is increased. It was from equally small beginnings that negro slavery took its rise in America; and unless great efforts be made to arrest its course, that nefarious institution will assuredly prove fatal to civilization in the southern parts of the African continent.

In advocating the establishment of a Confederation as the best means of putting an end to the two-fold curse of war and slavery, the writer has simply expressed the views of the most enlightened statesmen to whom the destinies of the Cape Colony have been entrusted. Those views have been endorsed by the Legislative Council of Natal, by the influential portion of the colonial press, and by the South African merchants resident in this country. It will of course be understood that the proposed Confederation can only be established with the voluntary consent of the several communities which would be invited to enter it.

7, ADAM STREET, ADELPHI,
    1st *February*, 1871.

A 2

2200300

THE DUTCH REPUBLICS OF SOUTH AFRICA.

LETTER I.

To R. N. FOWLER, Esq., M.P., Treasurer of the Aborigines' Protection Society.

MY DEAR SIR,—You have repeatedly brought the subject of the conduct and policy of the Dutch Boers towards the native tribes of South Africa under the notice of the members of the Aborigines' Protection Society, at its annual meetings. This is my apology for addressing you on a question which is perhaps as important as any now claiming the attention of those who are interested in the colonies of Great Britain. I refer to the practice of slavery in the Trans-Vaal Republic, to the violation of the treaty of 1852 which it involves, and to the external warfare and domestic tyranny of which it is the fruitful cause.

The Trans-Vaal Republic is bounded on the north by the Limpopo, where gold has recently been discovered ; on the south by the Vaal River, which separates the territory from the Orange Free State; on the east by a portion of the Drakensberg Mountains, and on the west by native tribes which still enjoy their independence. A glance at the map will suffice to show the vast superficial area—estimated at 100,000 square miles—over which 20,000 or 30,000 Boers claim to exercise jurisdiction. The other Dutch Republic—once known as the Orange River Sovereignty, and now designated the Free State—is a rich pastoral country, the southern boundary of which, the Orange River, partly constitutes the frontier line of the Cape Colony.

The two Republics of South Africa have a common origin, and, so far as their relations with the native races are concerned, a common history. The Dutch, in their own country, are the most peaceful and law-abiding of citizens; and those who have sat by their firesides in Holland find it difficult to understand why it is, that, as colonists, they have ever been cruel and mercenary. It is true that in this respect they are not singular ;

for in the northern island of New Zealand, in the pastoral districts of Queensland, and in the border territories of North America, men of the English race have vied with the Boers of South Africa in their selfish or inhuman treatment of the Aborigines. But, to the honour of the British Government, its influence in the collisions which so often take place between colonists and natives is generally exercised on the side of justice and mercy. It has more than once prevented the extermination of the Maories, and the wholesale confiscation of their lands; and to it is due the non-recurrence, for a period of fifteen years, of a Kaffir war—that gulf into which Chancellors of the Exchequer once periodically cast their surplus. As the hands of the Imperial Government are now tolerably clean, there is no inconsistency in appealing to them against the misdeeds of the Boers of South Africa.

It may be alleged that this is a proposed interference with the internal government of an independent state. It is true that the Dutch Republics of South Africa have enjoyed a separate existence for many years past. In the interval they have been as much masters of their own affairs as if the English had disappeared from the Cape; but it is not the less a fact, that their independence is based upon treaties which impose upon them (as well as upon us) certain well-defined obligations. As these obligations are just and reasonable—as indeed the non-observance of them involves, as a consequence, the subversion of public morality—the lapse of sixteen or of sixty years cannot lessen their force, or diminish the weight of the responsibility they entail. England may fairly consider the expediency of enforcing the treaty which has been broken; but of her moral right to enforce it there cannot be the shadow of a doubt.

The story of the wanderings of the Boers in the South-African wilderness is one of the most remarkable in the annals of colonization. Owning large numbers of Hottentot slaves, they resented the Act of Emancipation as a piece of grievous oppression towards themselves. Their fears were so worked upon by unscrupulous speculators, that many of them believed they would receive no compensation for the liberation of their slaves, and sold their claims on the Imperial Government at a ruinous loss. In 1835 there was a strong emigration movement among the disaffected, and an advance party, headed by Uys and Maritz, turned their backs upon the old colony, and, after encountering great hardships, entered Natal, which was then only colonized by a small settlement of Englishmen. In the following year they were joined by a considerable party, who may now be described as "the main body" of their discontented countrymen. The Dutch were soon strong enough to fight pitched battles with Dingaan, the Zulu king (who had massacred many of their number); and ultimately, in concert with Panda, they defeated him, and raised his rival to the throne. Upon their proclaiming a Batavian Republic, the Government of the Cape asserted its authority by force, and a state of civil war ensued. In 1843 the Boers formally surrendered their claim to Natal, and retired over the Drakensberg to the country now known as the Free State. There they united with bodies of their countrymen, who, from about the year 1826, had crossed the Orange River in seasons of drought. Some of the Boers, headed by Mr. Andries Pretorius, proceeded still farther into the interior, crossed the Vaal River, and took possession of the territory now known as the Trans-Vaal Republic. But the Imperial Government did not cease to regard them as British subjects, although it was not till 1848 that they were actually compelled to submit to the authority of the Governor of the Cape Colony.

In that year Sir Harry Smith proclaimed the Queen's sovereignty over the Orange River territory. The Committee of the Privy Council, in their report dated the 5th July, 1850, justify that act in these terms:—" In 1836 the emigrant Boers settled " themselves down in many parts of what is now called the Orange " sovereignty; they assumed absolute independence; established " a species of government for themselves; disputed native titles to "land; disclaimed being amenable to any native jurisdiction, " even when within the acknowledged territory of native chiefs; "and, in the result, it became apparent, that unless the British " Government interposed its authority, nothing but discord, " violence, and crime, and a total extinction of the rights of the " natives, must follow." The Committee further allege, that " to " adopt any other course than this would, in their opinion, be " productive of scenes of anarchy and bloodshed, probably ending "in the extinction of the African race over a wide extent of " country." Sir Harry Smith's policy was an unfortunate one. It was that of a soldier who, although not without good impulses, was always obstinate and often unteachable, and a stranger to that spirit of conciliation by which alone different races can be brought into subjection to one government. His proclamation led to a rebellion of the Boers. Sir Harry, who was more at home in the field than in the council-chamber, marched against the Boers, and completely routed them at a place called Boemplaats; but his measures for the internal government of the country were of a most crude and unsatisfactory character, and, on their failure, the British Government resolved to abandon the country. Those Englishmen who,.on the faith of the Governor's proclamations and of orders in Council, had emigrated to, or acquired property in, the territory across the Orange River, protested in vain against the haste with which the Imperial authorities ignored principles upon which, only a short time previously, they had considered themselves bound to act. Sir George Clerk was the Commissioner under whose personal direction British authority was withdrawn from the Trans-Orange territory. His arguments in favour of the policy of which he was the instrument were entirely drawn from considerations of self-interest, which might well have operated before the annexation, but which at a subsequent date could not fairly be regarded apart from the general interests of civilization in South Africa.

Those interests have greatly suffered by the separation of the Free State from the possessions of the British Crown. The Boers have shown how right the Committee of Council were in the special reasons they gave for proclaiming them British subjects. Not only has the country greatly retrograded, but it has engaged in a series of native wars of so pitiless and rapacious a character, that Sir Philip Wodehouse has, with the sanction of the Home Government, consented to acknowledge the Basutos as British subjects as the only means of preserving the remnant of their lands from robbery, and the tribe itself from destruction. And now, after a lapse of fourteen years, public opinion in South Africa is strongly in favour of retracing the backward step which was then taken.

Two years previously the bands of emigrant farmers who, under the "rebel" Pretorius, had crossed the Vaal River, and traversed a wide range of country (driving back or enslaving the natives), had negotiated a treaty by which they ceased to be British subjects. It is to the history of that treaty and its relation to the events which have followed, that I wish to call particular attention.

It is easy to sit in judgment on what experience has proved to be an error of policy; and, great as the mistake was, it was doubtless from the best possible motives that the independence of the disaffected Boers, who now form the two Republics of the Trans-Vaal and the Free State, was recognized. England found it difficult to govern scattered and distant communities of farmers who had defied her authority, and engaged in petty but vexatious rebellions, and whose country, moreover, promised to be a burden to the revenue. The Gordian knot was therefore cut by the entire severance of the territories occupied by the Boers from the British possessions at the Cape. While a constitution was yet denied to the Cape colonists, a handful of turbulent Dutch settlers in the interior obtained not only self-government, but independence; and, what was really to be deplored, they succeeded in making treaties with us which they have converted into instruments of oppression.

The convention with the Trans-Vaal Boers was drawn up on the 16th of January, 1852, between Major W. S. Hogge and Mr. C. M. Owen, Her Majesty's Assistant Commissioners for settling and adjusting the eastern and north-eastern boundaries of the colony of the Cape of Good Hope, and a deputation of emigrant farmers residing north of the Vaal River, the principal member of which was Mr. Andries Pretorius, then Commandant-General, and subsequently first President of the Republic of South Africa. The convention was ratified at Fort Beaufort on the 13th May, 1852, by General Cathcart, her Majesty's High Commissioner and the Governor of Cape Colony. The following are the only articles of the treaty which need be quoted :—

Art. I.—"The Assistant-Commissioners guarantee in the fullest manner, on the part of the British Government, to the emigrant farmers beyond the Vaal River, the right to manage their own affairs, and to govern themselves without any interference on the part of her Majesty the Queen's Government, and that no encroachment shall be made by the said Government on the territory beyond to the north of the Vaal River; with the further assurance that the warmest wish of the British Government is to promote peace, free trade, and friendly intercourse with the emigrant farmers now inhabiting, or who may hereafter inhabit, that country, it being understood that this system of non-interference is binding upon both parties.

III.—"Her Majesty's Assistant Commissioners hereby disclaim all alliances whatsoever, and with whomsoever, of the coloured natives north of the Vaal River.

IV.—"It is agreed that no slavery is, or shall be permitted or practised in the country to the north of the Vaal River by the emigrant farmers.

VI.—"It is agreed that no objection shall be made by any British authority against the emigrant Boers purchasing their supplies of ammunition in any of the British colonies and possessions in South Africa, it being mutually understood that all trade in ammunition with the native tribes is prohibited, both by the British Government and the emigrant farmers on both sides of the Vaal River."

I believe that from that day to the present the Boers of the Trans-Vaal have had no reason to impeach the good faith of the British Government. We have fulfilled our part of the compact to the letter: it remains to be seen whether they have fulfilled theirs.

Before consenting that the Boers should no longer be subjected to British authority, we were bound to provide for the security of the natives who were thus to be handed over absolutely to a new set of masters. Lord Grey had a just sense of the duty which our Government owed to the natives beyond the Vaal, to provide them with such assistance against the aggressions of the Boers as might lie in its power. Military aid was, of course, out of the question; but he was of opinion that the Government should, through its agents, promote a union of the tribes against their white enemies, and assist them, by the appointment of a suitable officer, to organize measures for their defence, and to settle down to agricultural pursuits. In a despatch addressed to Sir Harry Smith, on the 12th November, 1850, his lordship made this recommendation, but it was never acted upon, and indeed General Cathcart (the successor of Sir Harry) adopted rigidly a policy of non-interference as regarded both the Boers and the natives living to the north of the Vaal River.

It is true that the English Commissioners explicitly pledged the Boers to the abolition of slavery, and that this article of the treaty gives us, at the present time, an indubitable right to interfere with the domestic institutions of " the emigrant farmers." But the antipathy with which these persons regarded the native tribes, and the outrages of which they had been guilty, were too well known to allow it to be supposed that in this particular the treaty would be more than the dead letter it has ever since remained. It may, however, be urged that the British authorities did what they could, and that in making the prohibition of slavery one of the conditions upon which the independence of the Republic was based, they upheld a just principle, and, at the same time, gave to the Imperial Government a perpetual right to interfere in the interest of freedom. But it is not too much to affirm that any value which might be attached to Article IV. was wholly neutralized by the exceptional privileges conceded by Article VI. The Boers were permitted to purchase any quantity of ammunition from the colonial markets, while "all trade in "ammunition with the native tribes" was absolutely prohibited[1]. This was placing the lamb at the mercy of the wolf with a vengeance; and although it cannot be said that Article VI. has entirely accomplished its object, yet the effect of it has been to place the best weapons in the hands of the Boers, the worst in those of the natives; to give to the one party an unlimited supply of good ammunition, and to limit the other to a small and uncertain supply of inferior quality. If the Boers had acted justly by the natives, there perhaps would not have been much ground of complaint; but when it became manifest that they used their power to oppress and enslave the tribes in their neighbourhood, it was the duty of the British Government either impartially to close the markets against both parties, or to place the latter on equal terms.

The Trans-Vaal Boers signalized their independence by a systematic policy of outrage and violence. They expelled various Missionaries who were believed to be too friendly to the native races, and jealously excluded travellers from their country, even subjecting some of those who ventured to climb over the Chinese wall which Dutch exclusiveness had raised, to the imposition of fines and to yet more intolerable personal indignities. They enslaved the women and children among their captives under the name of "inboeking," or apprenticeship, and massacred many ancient tribes of Bushmen, whose very helplessness should have commanded that feeling of pity which the more warlike Kaffirs had failed to extort. The case of Dr. Livingstone is a striking example of the truth of these painful charges. In a memorial which that distinguished man addressed to Sir John Pakington on the 12th December, 1852, he stated that for eight years he had laboured among the Bakwains, who inhabited a country which was watered by the Kolobeng, Mariqua, and Limpopo rivers (about 24° south latitude and 26° east longitude). The efforts of the Missionary were crowned with success. Petty war-

---

[1] So thoroughly did the Boers understand the value of this concession, that they attached to the sale of gunpowder to the natives the penalty of death.

fare had ceased, and in all the regions around and beyond Lake Ngami, the Bakwains, under their chief Sechele, engaged in honest trade with their neighbours. No portion of the country ever belonged to the Boers. The road to it did not touch any of their possessions, and the Mission stations at Kuruman and Kolobeng were both about 100 miles west of the Dutch territory. Englishmen were the sole explorers of this distant region. Dr. Livingstone at the one station, and his not less eminent father-in-law, Mr. Moffatt, at the other, had made Christianity a power in the wilderness ; while English traders and English sportsmen had contributed their share towards rendering the people happy and prosperous. What followed is best described in Dr. Livingstone's own words : " Frequent attempts were made by the " Trans-Vaal Boers to induce the Chief Sechele to prevent the " English from passing him in their way north ; and, because " he refused to comply with this policy, a commando was sent " against him by Mr. Pretorius, which, on the 30th September " last, attacked and destroyed his town, killed sixty of his " people, and carried off upwards of 200 women and children. " I can declare, most positively, that, except in the matter of " refusing to throw obstacles in the way of English traders, " Sechele never offended the Boers by either word or deed. " They wished to divert the trade into their own hands. They " also plundered my house of property which would cost in " England at least 335l. They smashed all the bottles contain- " ing medicines, and tore all the books of my library, scattering " the leaves to the winds ; and, besides my personal property, " they carried off or destroyed a large amount of property be- " longing to English gentlemen and traders. Of the women and " children captured, many of the former will escape, but the latter " are reduced to a state of hopeless slavery. They are sold and " bought as slaves ; and I have myself seen and conversed with " such taken from other tribes, and living as slaves in the houses " of the Boers. One of Sechele's children is among the number " captured, and the Boer who owns him can, if necessary be " pointed out."

You will perhaps remember that Dr. Livingstone, in conversing with us on this painful episode in his career, mentioned that, when he subsequently travelled through the Republic, he saw in captivity among the Boers large numbers of Bechuana children, who had been educated in his own Sunday-schools, and afterwards torn from their homes by the ruffians who composed the Dutch commandos. Unfortunately, he was not so famous then as he is now ; and he obtained no redress, General Cathcart being of opinion that "the losses and inconveniences he had "sustained, did not amount to more than the ordinary occurrences "incidental to a state of war."

The fact was, that with a change of Governors there had come a change of policy, and the word had gone forth that we had nothing to do with the Boers except to maintain friendly relations with them. General Cathcart's unwillingness to involve his country in difficulties with the Trans-Vaal marauders may perhaps be attributed to a pacific disposition. If it were so, it is singular that the same Governor should have been so eager to plunge into a Kaffir war, which was as costly and calamitous as subsequent investigation proved it to have been unnecessary.

The Boers have not even the excuse of an unproductive soil for their raids upon their neighbours. The editor of the "Natal Mercury" has been good enough to send me an excellent description of the territory, which was written by a keen observer, who emigrated there from Natal seven years ago. This gentleman says that "from Zululand to Mendai, from "Vaal River to Zoutpansberg, it is a country which can produce "in any quantity wool, cattle, butter, corn, skins, feathers, "tobacco, coffee, sugar, cotton, fruit, spirits—not to speak of its "mines of coal, lead, iron, and most likely silver and gold."

It is therefore manifest that Nature has not been chary of her bounty in the territory of the Trans-Vaal, and that the Boers have really come into possession of what the foregoing writer calls "the finest stretch of land in all South Africa." Such a country, peopled by a hardy and industrious race, should be at once prosperous, and growing in prosperity. Instead of this, it is miserably poor, and public credit is at so low an ebb, that the paper currency (which is the only money circulating in the Republic) is worth next to nothing—articles being sometimes sold at 500 per cent. above their value, in order to enable the merchants to eke out a profit. A depreciated currency from being a consequence in its turn becomes a cause of poverty and social disorganization. This unhappy state of things takes its root in various causes. There are laws, but obedience to them is far from general. Little, if any, respect for authority exists. There are many high-sounding officials and departments, but there is

no unity of action among them, and they are mostly maintained
for show. One or two districts are in a state of open revolt
against a Government which is as weak and imbecile as it is
notoriously cruel. Education is all but neglected, and the
younger race of Boers are likely to be even more illiterate than
their fathers. The State does not support more than four public
schools, and the teachers in these complain that they cannot get
their salaries. Ridiculous stories are told of the sort of persons
—discharged soldiers and other luckless adventurers—who are
deemed qualified to teach the young idea how to shoot. But the
greatest source of demoralization—that, indeed, to which all
others are but as tributary streams—is the remorseless and fana-
tical hatred of the Boers towards the native tribes. Strange to
say, this passion has been exalted to a religious duty, and in the
Dutch commandos the intolerant spirit of the Crusader has
mingled with the cupidity of the buccaneer. To massacre the
men because they are heathen, and to enslave the children because they make cheap as well as useful house-servants and
farm-labourers—these are the chief features that distinguish
what may be called " the foreign" or Kaffir policy of the Boers.

For many years past the attention of the Aborigines' Protection Society has been directed to this subject—to the charges
preferred against the Boers, and to the denials and evasions
which they and their friends at the Cape have put forward in
their defence. My own personal connexion with this question
is not of recent date. So far back as the year 1856 I drew
up an address to Andries Pretorius, the father of the man who
now rules the Trans-Vaal. That address was a protest against
the violation of the fourth article of the treaty, and accused the
Boers of treating women and children " as sheep and oxen, or any
"other articles of merchandise."

During the intervening thirteen years we have repeatedly recurred to the same subject; and in December 1867, we forwarded
a memorial to Lord Stanley, giving as our reason for addressing
the Foreign instead of the Colonial Minister the fact that the
Boers had recently appointed a Consul to represent them in
London. Feeling that it was desirable to enumerate specific facts
rather than to make general allegations, we submitted to his lordship the following extract from a letter which was addressed to
the Society by Mr. William Martin, a highly-esteemed colonist of
Natal :—

"Maritzburg, Natal,
"June 7th, 1867.

"In the year 1864, after a sea voyage to Delagoa Bay, thirty-six hours from Natal, I took a 700 miles' trip to Zoutpansberg, Trans-Vaal Republic, which you will see on Hall's map. On my return I had charge of two waggons with ivory. I objected to any natives accompanying the waggons, but was told they were going to Natal for work. When we reached the capital, Pretoria, the natives (six in number) were forcibly seized and taken away from my protection by a Dutchman. I appealed to an official, the field cornet—who, I regret to say, was an Englishman—who assured me that the boys would run away, and that they were taken from me because they had not a pass, although the waggon had been searched for runaways before we reached the capital. Next day, on coming to the Vaal River boundary of the Free State, I was astonished to find that the brother of the Dutchman, who was a passenger in my cart, actually had one of the boys so forcibly seized. Two days afterwards he sent the poor wretch, on a Sunday, without allowing him any thing to eat, a long journey ahead, and took away his kaross or covering, although it was very wet. Next day the Vaal River was full when we crossed with a boat. The poor boy came to the bank, said he could swim, and, in coming through the stream, perished before our eyes, although every exertion was made to save him. I contend that this native lost his life by having been taken out of my protection, and I suppose the other five are still in bondage."

It appears that Lord Stanley did not consider that the subject belonged to his department, for he handed the memorial to the Duke of Buckingham, who then held the seals of the Colonial Office. It is a singular fact, that although that office professes to regard both the Dutch Republics as independent States, neither Lord Stanley, nor any other Foreign Minister, has ever condescended to hold diplomatic or political relations with them. These Republics, in fact, are, from the very nature of their position, mere dependencies of the Cape Colony. The British subjects in them have never been released from their allegiance; and in the case of the Orange Free State it is more than doubtful whether, from a constitutional point of view, the Crown had the power, without the consent of Parliament, to divest itself of a portion of the national territory. There is, indeed, good reason to believe that if the opinion of competent lawyers were obtained, it would be adverse to the legality of the extraordinary and irresponsible proceedings of the Colonial Office in this matter. I have been told, on high authority, that the late Duke of Newcastle did not conceal his opinion that the Government exceeded its powers, and that the only excuse for defending the step which had been taken was the difficulty of retracing it.

The memorial to which I referred before making this digression, urged upon the Colonial Minister the duty of requiring the Boers to fulfil the obligation to suppress the slave-trade, which they had voluntarily incurred as contracting parties to the treaty of 1852. Lord Alfred Churchill, a Vice-President of the Society, forwarded the memorial to its destination, and the official reply is worth reproducing :—

"Downing Street, 8th January, 1868.

"My Lord,

"I am directed by the Duke of Buckingham and Chandos to acquaint your lordship that his Grace has received from the Foreign Office the memorial signed by yourself and others, on behalf of the Aborigines' Protection Society, dated December, 1867, regarding the practice of Slavery in the Trans-Vaal Republic.

"He desires me to inform you that Sir P. Wodehouse expressed an opinion against interference in the year 1865, on the particular cases brought to light by Mr. Martin, and referred to in the memorial addressed by the Society to Lord Stanley in August last; but his Grace has satisfaction in apprising the Society that Sir P. Wodehouse, in the following year, on further facts coming to his knowledge, addressed vigorous remonstrances to the President of the Trans-Vaal Republic against the practices which were alleged of kidnapping children, and holding them in long terms of apprenticeship, tending to their enslavement; and that the President, in reply, announced that legal proceedings had been taken against certain offenders who had kidnapped children, and conveyed earnest assurances of the intention of his Government to repress slave-dealing and slavery.

"I am, my Lord,

"Your Lordship's obedient Servant,

"Frederick Elliot."

Although this letter is an admission that the charges preferred by the Society against the authorities of the Republic do not rest upon an isolated case, it yet presents Mr. Pretorius in the too flattering light of a Chief Magistrate who is scrupulously anxious to enforce the law and to ensure the observance of treaties. There is, however, too much reason to fear that in this matter Mr. Marthinus Wessel Pretorius is simply walking in the footsteps of his father, Mr. Andries Pretorius; and I am also afraid that Sir Philip Wodehouse was far too easily satisfied with "the earnest assurances" of the Trans-Vaal President. It would be some satisfaction to know what was the nature of the legal proceedings which are said to have been instituted against "certain offenders," and whether any body was imprisoned, fined, or even censured for indulging in a practice which the civilized world now condemns as a heinous crime. The fact is that there is no mystery or concealment about the so-called "apprenticeship" system. How could there be mystery or concealment when 4000 Kaffir "children" (many of them grown-up children) are held as slaves—although disguised as "apprentices"—by the Dutch farmers? To proceed fairly against "certain offenders" would be to arraign half the country at the bar, and to expect prosecutors, judges, and juries to convict themselves.

The Boers endeavour to conceal the real character of their institution under the euphemism of "apprenticeship." The theory which they seek to palm off on a credulous public is, that from motives of humanity they apprentice and exercise a paternal supervision over destitute Kaffir children. Tender-hearted Boers! They do not tell us who make the children destitute, who send out commandos for the express purpose of killing the parents in order to steal the offspring, who fix a price on "the black ivory" according to "the weight" (or age) of "the tusk." It would, perhaps, be too much to expect the Boers to impart information on these points, but they would at least be a shade or two more respectable if they ceased to play the hypocrite. I repeat that the Boers create the misery which they profess to alleviate; and I assert, without fear of disproof, that commandos are organized for the express purpose of capturing children to be converted into slaves, and that in all parts of the Republic a traffic in these human chattels is briskly carried on, the prices usually varying from twelve to twenty pounds per head.

Fortunately for the sake of humanity, the attention of right-minded persons in Natal and at the Cape has been drawn, of late years, to the proceedings of the Dutch settlers of the Trans-Vaal. Nor would it be right to withhold the credit which is due to citizens of the Republic who—not without considerable personal risk—have raised their voices and employed their pens in condemnation of the iniquities which have been perpetrated before their eyes. In the worst governed States there is always a minority who are keenly alive to injustice, and anxious to remove it as soon as they can exert the power, and that such a party exists in the Republic of South Africa is a great element of hope for the future of that country.

I regret that freedom of speech is so little respected in the Trans-Vaal that it would not be safe to mention the names of many of those who are prepared to revolutionize the native policy of the Boers. But Mr. G. W. Steyn, formerly Landdrost of Potchef-

B

stroom, had the courage to publish his name in connexion with
certain disclosures which appeared in the "Friend of the Free
State." If the reader will bear in mind the position of the writer,
he will not fail to be impressed by the testimony I am about
to quote:—

"Haassekraal, near Potchefstroom, Trans-Vaal,
"March 13th, 1866.

"You have already been made aware that loads of 'black ivory' (young
Kaffirs) are constantly hawked about the country, and disposed of like so many
droves of cattle. . . . . .

"I challenge President Pretorius to prove that the several young natives he
has in his service are orphans, or that one-fiftieth part of the (at least) 4000
natives sold here during the last fifteen years are such, unless they have been
deprived of their fathers, and perhaps mothers also, by the bullet of some
ruffian of a Boer. Will President Pretorius dare to deny that such is the manner in which hundreds of helpless children are annually made orphans, for the
sole purpose of benefiting the pockets of some miscreants? It is often asserted
that all these acts of woe are done to civilize the natives, and only amount to
the apprenticing of orphan children until they are twenty-five years old. Sup-
posing, for the sake of argument, that the hundreds of natives annually sold
are all orphans. How are these children to know when they are twenty-five
years old? and the means by which they may seek and obtain their freedom?
Their twenty-five is seldom if ever completed till death relieves them from the
bond of slavery. Call it what you will, it is slavery, by compulsory labour and
compulsory detention. President Pretorius belongs to a self-called religious
people, and he agrees with them in looking on the dark-skinned races as the
'accursed sons of Ham,' who only deserve the name of 'schepsels,' and who are
doomed by heaven to perpetual servitude. It is their opinion that by inflicting
slavery on the natives they are performing the will of God."

The statements made in this letter are sufficiently explicit, and
if borne out by subsequent inquiry (as they would have been if
an inquiry had been instituted), it is difficult to understand why
Governor Wodehouse should have been satisfied with the vague
assurances and promises of Mr. President Pretorius, or why the
Home Government did not insist upon the fulfilment of the treaty.

Some idea of the personal experiences of the captives may be
derived from four or five simple narratives which were taken down
from the lips of certain native women, and forwarded to me by a
gentleman in Natal, who has been zealous in his efforts to expose
the misdeeds of the Boers.

RACHEL'S STORY.

"I was taken by the Dutch when quite a babe. Our people
lived on the other side of Makapan's port. The Dutch fought

with them. Our fathers were beaten in the fight, and many of them were killed. Our mothers ran away with us, and hid in caves; but at last thirst compelled them to go in search of water. My mother and others were seen before they reached the water, and were shot, and we children were taken. The very little ones were put on horseback, while the bigger ones had to run on before, until we got to the Laager. At the division I fell to the lot of Mynheer——[2]. I stayed with him several years, and then he sold me to Mynheer——, with whom I stayed until I was grown up. The price he gave for me was 6*l.* and a cow in calf. I did not know, however, that I was sold until long afterwards. I was merely told to go and work for him. My first master was kind to me, but my second was very cruel.

"When I was grown up, my master sold me to a man (a native) who wanted me for a wife. He gave 6*l.* for me, but as he was a drunken fellow, and used me very cruelly, I ran away from him, and went back to my master. After some time I was again sold to the man with whom I now live. He also gave 6*l.* for me. Neither he nor the other were Kaffirs living up there, but were waggon-drivers from Natal. My master thus got 12*l.* for me. After taking me, my husband lived about two years amongst the Dutch, during which time I worked for different people, traders and others, up that way, and earned a cow; but when I came away with the man I am living with, I was not allowed to take it with me. It was kept by Mynheer——. When with Mynheer——, we lived in Pretoria, and during my stay there I saw many children brought down from beyond Zoutpansberg, and sold about town at from 3*l.* to 8*l.*, according to size. Some were sold for horses and cattle.

"At last my husband came down to Natal as waggon-driver, and we have lived here ever since. When at the Vaal River, on our way down, my husband's master told a little (black) boy to stay with a Dutchman living there until his return; and it was not till we were more than half-way down that we learnt that the boy had been sold. Children are very dear down at the Vaal River, as it is so far from where they are got. Children are what they call *apprenticed* out to the different people for a number of years, or until grown up. I never saw my papers, nor the papers

---

[2] The names of the woman's two masters are in my possession.

of any one else. When we are bartered or sold from one to another, we are not told of it, but are told that it is to stay for a little while. It is not until afterwards that we find we have been sold. When we think we have stayed long enough, and ask to be set free, we are whipped. I do not know of any one having got their liberty except by marriage to men not resident there. We are told that after we have served our time we will get paid for our work, but that we never do."

ADELA'S STORY.

"The country in which we lived before our people were scattered by the Dutch is near Zoutpansbsrg. I remember when I was taken, although very young at the time. There were others taken besides myself, some older and some younger. The Dutch surrounded our kraal while it was yet day, and set fire to the huts. The noise of the fire awoke us, and we ran out just as we were. The grown-up people who attempted to run out of the kraal were shot down, and the rest huddled together, surrounded by the Dutch on horseback. The children were then put together in one place, while the rest were made to go into the cattle kraal, which was built of stone, and were there shot at till they all fell down dead or dying. The Dutch then took us to their waggons, and we were divided amongst them. I fell to the lot of Mr. Van Zweel. My master often lived in town, and while there I used to see children brought down from Zoutpansberg, and sold for money or cattle. They did not use to hawk children about in this way when I was taken: this practice has taken place since; but one would sell to another, as occasion required. When I was about fourteen years of age my master sold me to a Natal Kaffir waggon-driver for 30l. I came down here with him, and have lived with him ever since. He was at that time, and still is, waggon-driver to the Messrs. Barrett of this city."

SOPHIA'S STORY.

"I was born in Zululand. When I was still quite young the Dutch came and made war against our king. They were generally victorious, and then did their best to capture the children and cattle. I remember the time I was taken captive. There had been a great fight, and our fathers were beaten. Our mothers fled with us, and hid in the kloofs, but the white men saw where we went to, gave chase, and we were taken. Our mothers were very sorrowful, and cried very much. They attempted to follow on behind, but the Dutch told them to go back, or they would shoot them. My mother followed for some distance, but at last I lost sight of her. She could not keep up with the horses. As we grew up and began to understand the Dutch and their ways, we were told that we had to serve an apprenticeship, and would then get wages. After we had served many years their President told us that we had served long enough, and ought to be set free or get wages; but we did neither. Finding that I never would be free so long as I lived with the Dutch, I made up my mind to try and escape to where the English lived, as I had heard of them from the Natal Kaffir waggon-drivers and leaders, who came into the country with their masters to trade or hunt. So one evening I ran away, and travelled during the night, until I got to where an Englishman lived, near the border. He had a Dutch wife, who knew me. She was a good woman, and hid me until her husband was ready to go down to Natal with his waggon, and then I came with him. I am a member of the Wesleyan Society, and was converted under the late Rev. Mr. Pearse."

ODELA'S STORY.

" Odela says, when she was very little the Dutch came before day-break, and those who ran away were shot down. Old people were shot down, the Dutch not waiting to see whether they were living or not. The big people were separated from the others, and driven into stone kraals. Since living amongst the Dutch she often saw commandos go out, and the people return with children taken from their homes in the same way as she was. She often saw Commandant Schoeman and President Pretorius at Zoutpansberg. Another woman from Zoutpansberg, who resided last at Pretoria, also alleges, in addition to the foregoing, that whilst at Pretoria she often saw waggons with children, who were sold to the people about there, 6l. and 12l. being the price asked for children, according to their age. . . . . If the people are sent by the chief at the order of the commandant, they get a sheepskin a month, or a heifer a year. If the chief could not prevail on the people to come, or from some other cause, the Dutch would say he was getting impudent, and required a lesson. This was their excuse for assembling a commando.

"By Utrecht (adjoining Natal) the Dutch buy children for dogs."

LEAH'S STORY.

"I was born in the Trans-Vaal, in the district of Marico, a fine country, where we lived happily. But when I was about seven years of age the Dutch made war on our people, and I and many other children were taken captive.

"My father was one of Mozilikatse's people, and I left Zulu-land with him, in company with a great many others. This was in the days of the great king Chakar, who then ruled in Zululand. The Dutch fought often with our chief, Mozilikatse. I remember the time when I and others were taken. It was about noon when we heard the firing, or the thunder as we called it. We children did not know what it meant, but our mothers told us that it was the white people come to kill us, and that they had come on horses, although we young people did not know what horses were. In a short time we fled. I and my sister went away with a young woman, and hid ourselves in a bush. The country was a large plain, covered with thorn-bush, with mountains in the background. We had not been long in our hiding-place when two young men from our army came to us, and sought to hide from their pursuers; but it was too late, as they had been seen to enter, and immediately after three white men rode up and ordered us to come out. We at once obeyed. The two young men were shot as soon as they were seen. We two children were taken up on horseback, while the young woman was made to run on in front. We were then taken to the waggons. After a few days the white men inspanned their oxen and started on their way to Laager, taking a great number of cattle, so many as not to be counted, and a very great number of children, great and small. On the way cattle were killed for our consumption, but we had no heart for it. Some ate a little, some ate nothing, and some vomited what they did eat. A few made their escape by the way and hid themselves, but I can't say what became of them, whether they met with friends or wild animals, it being a country where lions abounded. After many days (perhaps fifteen) we arrived at the Laager, and there the Dutch found their wives and children. They were living in tents and waggons, and rejoiced very much to see their husbands return with so many children and cattle. In the evening I went to seek my little sister, but they would not let me go. I was very unhappy, being alone amongst strangers, for here the Dutch separated, each family going to their own home. My master had several others besides myself as his share, also cattle, sheep, and goats. I lived with my master about six years, and got food and clothes. The dress we wore was a single one of cotton, reaching from the shoulder to below the knees. Some got no dress at all, only a piece of old stuff tied round the breast, and a narrow strip round the loins.

"At the end of this time my master came down to Pieter-maritzburg with produce, and brought me with him. The night before his return home I ran away, and have continued to live free ever since. I was converted under the late Rev. Mr. Pearse, of the Wesleyan Society, and have since married. I am now the mother of five children. I take in washing.

"Pietermaritzburg, Natal. 22nd Jan., 1868."

No language of mine could add to the pathetic interest of these narratives. They bear the impress of truth, and are by no means the most harrowing that might have been selected.

A gentleman whose name has been communicated to me states that on visiting a Boer village last year he was shown the books of a storekeeper in which he read the following entry:—"One "large ivory tusk, 12l." "This is the plan adopted for booking "the purchase or sale of little boys and girls, commonly called "'black ivory,' or 'little goods.' An amount of 12l. was owing "by a young man from Natal, who had removed his purchase "300 miles, and a brisk trade was going on." The same gentle-man was asked one day to purchase some "black ivory." The children in this instance were owned by a German trader, who had placed them alongside his waggon in the main street, and was openly offering them for sale at a short distance from the Landdrost's house. These children, ten in number, had been exchanged for horses.

The practice of slavery by the Boers has naturally arrested the attention of the Cape Parliament; and in July, 1868, Mr. Godlonton moved for the production of all the correspondence on the subject which had passed between the Governor and in-habitants of the Trans-Vaal Republic and Her Majesty's Govern-ment. Mr. Godlonton strongly condemned the traffic, and especially urged that as the majority of the people in the Trans-

Vaal Republic were British subjects, it was the duty of the Imperial Government to interfere.

At the same time Mr. John Robinson[3] made a similar motion in the Natal Legislature. This gentleman emphatically declared that slavery existed in the Trans-Vaal with the knowledge and connivance of the Government. He ridiculed the notion that it was a system by which benevolent farmers made provision for destitute children, and declared that " war parties were despatched " expressly to get these children, and plunder the tribes against " whom they went out." Mr. Robinson, in proof of his statement, appealed to a report of a Commission which had been appointed by the Volksraad at the close of the year 1867, and to a remarkable meeting which was held at Potchefstroom in May last.

The proceedings of this meeting confirm in every essential particular the allegations which have been made in the Cape and Natal papers with reference to the pretended apprenticeship of destitute children, and certainly there could be no better evidence of the truth of these statements than the testimony of respectable citizens of Potchefstroom, who could have no possible interest in misleading the public. The Rev. Mr. Ludorf dwelt on the injury which was done to commerce by the incessant levying of commandos. " Our door-posts," he said, " were polluted with " blood, and nothing could efface those stains but the punishment " of the guilty." Mr. James Evans, the member for Potchefstroom, said that " the murders and plunderings reported in the ' Staats " Courant ' as having been committed were but a fractional part " of the crimes that had been perpetrated." Mr. Steyn remarked that " he had in former days fearlessly met the enemy, but he " must candidly own that in such a cause he was a coward, for " it was an unrighteous cause, and we could not expect that the " blessing of Providence would rest on our arms." An important speech was made by Mr. J. H. Roselt, the editor of the " Trans-Vaal Argus," which is the only newspaper published in the Republic. This gentleman, who with noble indifference to personal consequences, has refused to serve on commandos which have been organized for kidnapping purposes, and who, for calling a spade a spade, has more than once exposed himself to the risk

[3] It is no secret that Mr. Robinson is the author of two admirable articles in the "Westminster Review," which have given the British public a view of South African politics as comprehensive as it is accurate.

of a prosecution for treason, observed that "when Majatje, the
" Meidkaptem, and a friendly tribe, was lately attacked by
" Schoeman's commando, no less than 103 children were found
" destitute, together with seven belonging to another kraal ; that
" of these children he had been informed thirty-seven had been
" disposed of by lot ; and he would therefore like to know what had
" become of the remaining sixty-six, for they had disappeared in
" a most miraculous and mysterious manner." There was some
difference of opinion in the meeting as to whether the law should
prohibit Landdrosts from apprenticing destitute children to
the burghers who served in the commandos. In other words,
many of those who raised their voices against slave-hunting, as
now carried on, were not averse to slave-holding, if it could be
practised in a less objectionable manner. One old Dutchman,
Jan Taljaard by name, was for destroying the whole system root
and branch; but Daniel Van Vooren, a Boer of the sanguinary
school, grimly remarked that, " if they had to clear the country
" (het land schoonmaken), and could not have the children they
" found, he would shoot them." Mr. Robinson was surely
justified in regarding these statements as conclusively proving
that slavery was an established institution in the Republic ; and
in calling on the government of Natal to repudiate the iniquitous
proceedings of the Boers, especially as he said he had reason to
know that some of our countrymen were encouraging the
system.

I wish now to ask your attention to a portion of the territory
which has gained an unenviable notoriety for its turbulence, its
wars with the natives, and its kidnapping expeditions.

Zoutpansberg is one of the finest districts in South Africa: it
is the chief source of "the black ivory" trade, and the key to the
traffic with the interior in ivory, ostrich feathers, and other
valuable commodities. For years past this district has been the
scene of constant warfare. In the end the tables have been
turned, and the Boers have sustained a series of reverses. Owing
to the military incompetence of their leaders, as well as to the
pusillanimity of some of the men and the disgust of others who
have been pressed into the service, they have been repeatedly
forced to retreat, and have seen some of their outlying settlements
devastated and abandoned. In consequence of these reverses,
the Volksraad appointed a Commission to institute an inquiry.
Their report has been published in the "Argus," and it is no

exaggeration to say that it convicts the Boers on their own testimony of having committed the very worst excesses. It appears that the government is represented at Zoutpansberg by several superintendents of native affairs, one of whom is a certain Signor Albasini, the Portuguese Consul, who is described as the evil genius of that part of the country. The great chief Mozela made a demand on Albasini for the delivery up to him of a lesser chief named Monene, whom he accused of having robbed some of his people. Although it was notorious that Mozela's purpose was to murder Monene, the Dutch authorities were quite prepared to surrender him, Mozela having prohibited elephant-hunting in the district of Chinquini, until his enemy had been delivered into his hands. Monene was apparently fast in the grip of one Field Cornet Stephanus van Rensenburg, but he succeeded in making his escape, and after having fled from one tribe to another, found a refuge with the chief Swaas. The Boers, in his flight, with suicidal recklessness, turned their arms against various tribes on the mere suspicion of having sheltered him. For example : " Commander Venter states that he attacked " Paco and Lahotto because he had heard that Monene had taken " refuge there, but after having routed these chiefs, he discovered " that Monene had gone to Swaas." A commando was sent against Magor, another Kaffir chief, on the false pretext (so the Commissioners declare it to have been) that he was implicated in a plot to massacre the whites. " Magor was told to come down " from the mountain and bring his taxes with him. Unless he " came of his own accord he could not be reached; but as his " personal safety had been promised him, and relying as he did " upon that promise, he came down from the mountain, thus " placing himself in the lion's den, bringing his taxes with him, " which consisted of between 200 and 300 head of cattle. No " sooner, however, had these taxes been secured, and the victim " in their power, than he was placed in confinement, and the same " night murdered, whilst his tribe was destroyed by those blood- " hounds, the Knobnoses, who are exclusively under the command " of Albasini, and ready at any time to carry out his orders, " whatever their nature." Another victim was Tabaan (or Tabuna), who, it is said, regularly paid his taxes to the government. He, too, was murdered, his cattle carried off, and the women and children of his tribe made captive. This is the mode by which the latter generally become destitute and are reduced

to such straits that, according to the benevolent theories of
Mr. Marthinus Wessel Pretorius, it is an act of charity to enslave
them. The Commissioners offer strong testimony as to the com-
plicity of the government in these misdeeds, and as to their
having successfully shielded the evil-doers against the punishment
due to their offences. The Commission further alleges as the
cause of the present deplorable state of Zoutpansberg, " that
" certain officials and officers, who have from time to time broken
" the law, by wilful neglect of duty, abuse of the power entrusted
" to them, and other misdemeanours, have not been punished
" for so doing, as also that by adopting a wrong course of treat-
" ment of the native tribes at that time both peaceable and subject
" to the government, many of these Kaffir tribes at length became
" insubordinate."

It must not be supposed that these facts represent a condition
of society which has passed away. That the contrary is the case
is shown by a letter dated July 25, 1868, in which one Mr. Michael
Lynch describes the attempted storming of Mapela's mountain,
and the disastrous retreat of the Boers on that occasion. He
adds:—

" At Mapela's a number of women and children came into the pos-
" session of the commando; the number, however, I am unable to
" state, nor do I know what afterwards became of them. We
" were well supplied with ammunition up to the time the com-
" mando left, when the surplus was handed over to the different
" field-cornets. To the best of my knowledge and belief, not
" more than 100 Kaffirs were killed at Mapela's. Most of the
" wounded men on our side were so wounded in their disgraceful
" retreat."

Mr. Michael Lynch does not know what became of the women
and children. A correspondent of mine, writing from the Trans-
Vaal territory on the 26th of August 1868, leaves little doubt as
to their ultimate destination. He says that, for the present, they
will remain in the hands of a friendly chief, but that when matters
become a little more settled the Boers will go and fetch them,
and make them slaves. He states that, besides these captives,
other children were also taken. " An inquiry was instituted to
" ascertain whether the parents of these children were alive.
" Much to the disappointment of many of the officers who com-
" posed the krysgraad (council of war), the parents were dis-
" covered in a neighbouring kraal, and at a short distance from

"the camp; but this did not signify. It was alleged that the "distance was too great to send the children to their parents. "They will, therefore, either become 'prisoners of war,' or 'des- "titute apprentices'—in reality, slaves." The same correspon- dent calls my attention to a letter from a Dutch Boer, published in the "Argus," in which reference is made to the case of a native woman who was deliberately shot dead, that some ruffian might gain possession of her child, "who now falls under the "class called 'destitute,' and as such becomes an apprentice or "slave."

No wonder that the farmers in this region have deserted their homesteads; that the expenses of these miserable commandos have ruined the exchequer; that, in the language of a petition to the Volksraad, "whilst the mechanic is compelled to accept "a pound note at twenty shillings, he has to pay it away for "goods at one-third to one-half less';" and that, in a word, the whole country is going down the hill.

"So pays the devil his liegeman brass for gold."

It is manifest from these various statements, and from many others which might be quoted, that the Boers are constantly engaged in aggressive warfare with the natives, and that their kidnapping propensities have made them more savage than the savages—more ruthless than the native owners of the soil, whom they are doing their best to destroy or to enslave. It is equally clear that slavery is not an isolated practice, but it is supported by all classes of the people, from the President down to the most uncouth Boer residing on the uttermost borders of civilization. It is therefore marvellous that Mr. Pretorius should have found it so easy to throw dust into the eyes of Sir Philip Wodehouse, and that Mr. Cardwell should have so readily acquiesced in that "do nothing" policy, which is not always honourable because it is convenient.

I have already quoted Dr. Livingstone's memorial to Sir John Pakington, in which he gives an account of the attack which the Boers made on his Mission station; and the reader who desires to know the doctor's latest testimony on this subject would do well to refer to the first volume of his travels. Mr. Chapman is

---

⁴ The Boers cannot say with Mrs. MacCandlish in "Guy Mannering," "As lang as siller's current, folk maunna look ower nicely at what king's head's on't;" for neither silver nor gold has any place in the Trans-Vaal currency.

another traveller who speaks with the authority derived from a lengthened residence in the Trans-Vaal country. His testimony is of great value:—

"The Boers from time to time organized against them [the native tribes] commandos, as they are termed, being levies in arms of all the able-bodied men under the command of the field-cornet of the district. It was easy work for those men, well-mounted, inured to hardships in their hunting expeditions, and expert in the use of fire-arms, to carry devastation wherever they went. The cattle were swept off, villages burnt, the inhabitants massacred, and what was perhaps the worst feature in the case, the women and children, and often the men, were dragged away to become forced labourers—in fact, slaves—on the Dutchmen's farms. Against such attacks the natives could offer little resistance; but they retaliated, when opportunity offered, by waylaying and murdering small parties of the Boers, and frequently by lifting their cattle. The root of the evil now lies in the assumption of the Trans-Vaal Boers that all the country from the Orange River north, to an extent unlimited, and from sea to sea, belongs to them, and only waits the occupation which their roving propensities, and the increasing demands of pasture for their cattle, will necessitate. . . . . . The Boers also purchase many native children, who, with those captured in their wars with the tribes, remain in a condition of slavery until released by death. *I have had many of these unfortunate beings offered me, either in exchange for a horse, a quantity of merchandize, or in liquidation of a debt,* and have often been tempted to purchase one or other to redeem it, for charity's sake; but, on the other hand, there was something so repulsive to my feelings in the very idea of such a transaction, that I was compelled to refrain from doing the good I had intended. Two of these wretched little creatures were sold and re-sold, and afterwards redeemed by an agent of Messrs. Young and Co. (Jung and Co.) of Natal. . . . . But not only are children thus acquired: men and women of any age, taken by illegitimate means, are sold or exchanged for cattle or goods."

When I come to quote the resolutions which have been passed by the Legislative Council of Natal, it will be found that the statements I have made are supported by the strongest official testimony; for nothing could be more emphatic than the declarations of this branch of the Colonial Legislature. It will be seen that Sir Philip Wodehouse has never called the facts in question, but that, in reply to the appeal which was addressed to him, he made the humiliating confession that he could not interfere with any prospect of success. Sir Philip's view of the impossibility of putting down a trade "which the Boers must find to be very "tempting and profitable," would have justified a feeling of exultation in the breast of every owner of a slave barracoon on the East Coast of Africa.

But the official evidence goes much farther back than the

month of August last year. So long ago as December, 1855, Mr. Surtees, the Arbitrator in the Mixed Commission Court at the Cape, addressed Lord Clarendon as follows:—"In 1852 a " treaty was concluded between Sir George Cathcart and the " Trans-Vaal Boers, when their independence being recognized, " one of the articles stipulated that slavery should not exist in " the Trans-Vaal territory ; but the treaty omitted to provide any " mode by which the stipulation was to be enforced. Since the " conclusion of that treaty, as before, it has been constantly ru- " moured throughout this colony that the children of the Bush- " men and other natives were kept in slavery by the Boers, some- " times being obtained by barter, but often by force. The pro- " clamation of Pretorius has now established the truth. I am " bound to state to your Lordship my conviction that this evil, so " long unchecked, and at length openly acknowledged, as it is " of no light character, is one that calls for a speedy remedy ! " In these views he was sustained by the high authority of Mr. Shepstone, and subsequently by that of Sir George Grey, who was instructed by Mr. Labouchere to make a full report on the subject to the home government. His Excellency, in a despatch dated the 22nd May, 1866, writes like a statesman, and also displays a sagacity which is not far removed from prescience.

" 'On another point,' said the Governor, 'connected with this subject, I have formed opinions which I ought to express. The treaties at present existing between ourselves and the Trans-Vaal Republic and the Orange Free State amount in fact to this—that we must enter into no treaties with native tribes ; that we must allow no native tribes to obtain arms and ammunition ; that we must allow the two Republics to obtain such arms and ammunition as they require. I think that power ought to be given to me in some measure to modify these treaties, if a necessity for my doing so arises. In my mind these treaties amount, on our part, to a declaration that we abandon the coloured races to the mercy of the two Republics. If, from a determination to embark in no further operations in South Africa, we had resolved to remain strictly neutral, I could understand it. But in this case we do much more than remain neutral, and if, as is now asserted by many well-informed persons, a general combination of the coloured tribes is being attempted to be formed against us, I fear that these treaties have naturally had some influence upon the chiefs who have joined the confederacy. It would be well, I think, to consider how far such stipulations consist with the honour and greatness of Great Britain ; or, at least, whether there are not many circumstances under which such stipulations ought not to be maintained.' "

Sir George Grey was right. Our own interests, as well as those of the natives have suffered from the engagements which we recklessly entered into in 1852 and 1854; and in thus " abandon-

" ing the coloured races to the mercy of the two Republics " we
became morally responsible for the evil that ensued. To withdraw the restraints of law and authority from communities which
were so largely composed of ignorant and unprincipled men was
bad enough; but to hold no political relations whatever with the
natives to the north either of the Orange or of the Vaal River,
was simply to announce to the Boers that they were at liberty to
follow the bent of their own inclinations, and to commit murder
and rapine at will. That this interpretation has been put upon
the two Conventions is manifest from the fact, that since we have
interfered in Basutoland to save the natives from destruction,
the Free State Volksraad has protested against our conduct as a
breach of the treaty. While ignoring every principle of morality
themselves, they are not slow to hold us to the letter of our bond.
I do not know whether Sir Philip Wodehouse replied to the
charge; but without being a master of invective, or of the art
of satirical writing, he might have confounded his adversaries
with such an answer as would have stung them to the quick [5].

The truth is that Great Britain has assumed duties and responsibilities in South Africa which she cannot abandon. She cannot,
with honour, cease to protect the natives whom she has conquered,
and whose territories—so far as it has suited her own pleasure
and interest—she has seized. From the time that she subjugated
the Kaffirs and extended her dominion into the interior of that
great continent, which is no longer a *terra incognita*, she came
under a bond to impart to them a superior civilization. She had
a perfect right to consult her own ideas of policy when the question simply was whether she should continue to recognize the
Boers as subjects of the British Crown. But when she surrendered her sovereignty over her Dutch subjects she could not with
justice withdraw her protecting arm from the native tribes when
they were assailed by the lawless violence of men whom she had
released from their allegiance. The fact that, in the treaties
which she entered into with the two Dutch Republics, she directly
stipulated with them that the enslavement of the coloured race
should for ever be prohibited was in itself a recognition on her
part of this paramount duty. The treaty has been shamelessly
violated: it is her duty to enforce it, and to insist that the
plighted words of nations shall not become " false as dicers'

---

[5] *Vide* a valuable pamphlet entitled "British Rule in Africa; a Collection of
Official Documents and other Correspondence, &c." Cape Town, 1868.

" oaths." The Trans-Vaal Boers are in league with the Portuguese slave-traders on the East Coast. Together they foment
those inter-tribal wars which are the great feeders of the external
slave-trade, and make the European "soul merchant" a far more
revolting being than the lowest type of the negro race. The
Trans-Vaal slaveholders have been accustomed to buy a portion
of the "black ivory" from the Portuguese, who are well content
to find a convenient market for their human chattels. It is possible that Portugal may assist her accomplice to obtain a port in
Delagoa Bay, but at present the Boers can only carry on their
intercourse with the outer world through British territory. We
are masters of the sea, and masters also of those markets (at
least of powder and shot) from which the Boers draw their supplies. Long ago Dr. Livingstone pointed out that we might soon
bring the offenders to terms by prohibiting, under heavy penalties, the sale to them of arms and ammunition, or by declaring
free trade in those articles as respects the natives, and no longer
giving to the stronger party a monopoly of the means of destruction. It is probable that so extreme a measure would be unnecessary if England, in the person of her representative, the
Governor of the Cape Colony, would only exert her moral influence on the side of justice. If the facts are denied, let her
Majesty's representative despatch a Commission of Inquiry to
Potchefstroom, where abundant evidence to prove the truth of
the allegation against the authorities and people of the Republic will be forthcoming. But the facts are not denied. The
plea set up by the Boers is, that the children they enslave are
destitute, and their enforced labour prompted by motives of
humanity. The facts which the Boers conceal are, that the
children have been made orphans by Dutch rifles, and that the
Kaffir cattle (which might have supplied them with food) have
been carried off to swell the colonial herds.

The discovery of gold in the country which lies beyond the
north-west boundary of the Trans-Vaal Republic promises to
revolutionize this region of Africa. If half that is said concerning the extent and productiveness of the new gold-fields be true,
and if the physical difficulties consequent upon labouring in so
remote a region are overcome, the establishment of a British
colony in a part of Africa hitherto known only to a few adven-
turous explorers, is a matter of tolerable certainty. That gold is
to be had on the banks of the Tatin (a tributary of the Lim-

popo) is proved by the report of the miners who have already commenced operations; and it is also certain that the quartz is rich in the proportion of the precious metal which it will yield to machinery. It is true that the journey is 700 or 800 miles from Natal, but there are few perils to encounter by the way, and new and more direct routes will probably be opened. It seems probable that gold exists in large quantities to the eastward and on other tributaries of the Limpopo. It is notoriously worked on a river called the Bepi, where the natives pound the quartz, and then convey the precious residuum to Sofala and barter it with the Portuguese for cattle, beads, and blankets. To Herr Mauch, the enterprising German traveller, belongs the credit of the immediate discovery of these gold-fields, but numerous old workings testify to the antiquity of the knowledge now newly regained. The Natal journals believe that Sofala is identical with the Ophir of Solomon, and concerning which another sacred writer has said, " Then shalt thou lay up gold as dust, and the gold of Ophir as " the stone of the brooks." It is worthy of remark that Milton thus fixed the locality of the famous port—

> "And Sofala, thought Ophir, to the realm of Congo."

Tradition, however, only points to Sofala as it has pointed to Arabia, Malacca, and India. Herr Mauch has gone to explore the ancient ruins which are said to exist to the west of Sofala, and if the old story, that there is in that country a strong fortress of unknown origin and pre-historic antiquity, should prove to be well founded, he may chance to shed some light on the claim of Sofala to the honour of identity with the Ophir of the Bible. Be this as it may, the courageous German, like many contemporary travellers, is doing his best to wipe away the old reproach to which a great satirist gave witty expression:—

> " Geographers in Afric maps
> With savage pictures fill their gaps;
> And o'er uninhabitable downs
> Place elephants for want of towns."

It is curious that, during a recent visit to Europe, Father Sabon, of Durban, discovered in one of the libraries of Paris a Jesuit Missionary work of the date of 1620, in which the precise situation of the Victoria gold-fields is indicated. But whether Sofala and Ophir are the same or not, it cannot be denied that the discovery of a gold region beyond Natal and the Trans-Vaal Republic marks a new era in the history of African civilization.

c

The manner in which Mr. President Pretorius received the intelligence of the discovery was characteristic. He at once issued a proclamation, annexing a vast tract of country, as far to the north-west as Lake Ngami, and of course including the entire area in which the precious metal is likely to reward the patient labour of the digger. The Portuguese Cousul-General at Cape Town complained that the proclamation added to the Trans-Vaal a slice of territory which had formed part of the dominions of Portugal since 1546. Sir Philip Wodehouse has also asked Mr. Pretorius for an explanation, and the chiefs, whose territories are thus coolly taken possession of on paper, are even more entitled to one. Nothing could more forcibly illustrate the temper of the Boers towards the natives than this proceeding. When Mr. Pretorius took up his pen to write his proclamation, he probably had no more idea of there being a right and a wrong in the transaction than Ahab had when he laid hands on Naboth's vineyard. The Maories have a saying, that the European rat has already devoured the Maori rat, but the European rat in New Zealand is a creature of moderate appetite compared with the Trans-Vaal vermin.

Mr. Pretorius, however, is powerless to give effect to his proclamation, and its only result has been to expose the weakness and cupidity of the Boers. The British flag has been raised at the Victoria gold-fields, and Macheng, the chief to whom the country belongs, has expressed his desire to have the benefit of British protection. His tribe—the Bamangwato—are said to be "a quiet and kindly people," among whom " the traveller, the trader, and the hunter find no dangers, and " expect no heavy losses." Macheng, in a letter to Sir Philip Wodehouse, invites his Excellency to come and occupy the gold country, and to govern the gold-diggers in the name of the Queen of England. He says that the Trans-Vaal Government, through Commandant Jan Viljoen, had desired him to hand over the district to the Republic, but that he had declined to consider these overtures until he had heard from Sir Philip. Macheng has a laudable fear of the Boers, and would greatly prefer to see English authority established in his gold-fields. It is still more gratifying to know that our conduct towards the Kaffirs for many years past justifies the good opinion in which we are held by the Bechuana chief.

It is perhaps as easy to exaggerate as it is to undervalue what are called " the signs of the times ;" but it really seems as if events were now conspiring to realize the dream of a South-African con-federation. Formerly the expansion of British power was inse-parably associated with a levelling policy of annexation, and one stereotyped system of government. To find rich farms for needy colonists, and to rule the natives after a strictly British fashion, were the two ideas which filled the brains of even able adminis-trators. The theory was, that the natives must either submit to be so governed or die, and, in fact, thousands of them actually pre-ferred death to this sort of submission. Writing of a period by no means very remote, Lord Macaulay says, " The only barbarian " about whom there was no wish to have any information was the " Highlander." The Kaffirs were regarded with a somewhat dif-ferent manifestation of the same hateful prejudice. To prove that this feeling was hateful, it is not necessary to paint the untutored savage in roseate hues. The Kaffirs, like the Highlanders, have a higher capacity for improvement than too many of the colonists suppose. It also unfortunately happened that many of the earlier rulers of the Cape, who were military men, took a professional view of these warlike tribes, and considered them as only fit to be food for powder. Old errors are passing away with the generation whose selfish purposes they served. Peace now reigns, as it has long reigned, on the British frontier. How much of this is due to the efforts of men like Mr. Shepstone, the Native Secretary of Natal, and Mr. Charles Brownlee, the Gaika Commissioner, it would be hard to say ; but these enlightened officials belong to a class of colonial statesmen who prefer to rule by reason rather than by force, and who manage to avert danger by the keenness with which they scent it from afar, and by the promptitude and energy with which they guard against its approach. Great Britain is now sometimes magnanimous as well as just ; for it is not too much to affirm, that by her timely interference on behalf of the Basutos and the devoted French Missionaries in Basuto-land she has prevented the torch of Christianity from being ex-tinguished in a heathen land, and, at the same time, saved many thousands of natives from enslavement or extermination. In Natal, since the Zulus were beaten in open fight, the colonists have been at peace with the natives, and the latter have, in their turn, exhibited an amenability to restraint, and a willingness to labour, which might have taught the Boers a useful lesson if they had been willing to learn. To unite the diverse tribes and com-

munities of South Africa in one confederation may appear a
Quixotic enterprise, but the attempt is worth the best efforts of
the wisest statesmanship we can command. It will, however,
prove impracticable if, without regard to differing circumstances,
the whole country is sought to be governed on one model. The
wise ruler will endeavour to discover the means by which English,
Dutch, and native institutions may continue in operation while
the authority of British law and the supremacy of the Crown are
inflexibly maintained. It would take time and patience, and
great administrative skill, to carry out so great an undertaking,
but the achievement would be worthy of many trials and
sacrifices.

At present the functions of the Governor of the Cape Colony
as High Commissioner are as anomalous as those of a French
Minister would be, who attempted to regulate the affairs of the
Algerian frontier without the intervention of a Governor-General.
Living a thousand miles from Natal, his knowledge of what is
going on in the Trans-Vaal Republic is ignorance itself, as compared with the information which is constantly within the reach of
the officials and people of that colony. He is also otherwise ham-
pered in the discharge of his important functions. Sir Philip
recently expressed his inability, for want of funds, to send an
agent to the gold-fields, the discovery of which has occasioned so
much stir among the white populations of South Africa; and
even if the Natal legislature found the means, it is doubtful
whether the government of that colony would not exceed its
powers if it despatched an embassy on its own account. It is
therefore not surprising that the people of Natal should be dis-
satisfied, and their legislature prompt to give expression to the
public discontent. The resolutions passed by the Legislative
Council on the 10th of August, 1868, are so important that it is
necessary to give them *in extenso* :—

"1. That in the opinion of this House the office of High Commissioner, as
exercised at present in relation to this colony, is inimical to the maintenance of
the prestige and influence of her Majesty's Government amongst the native
tribes of South-East Africa, and the House is guided to this conclusion by the
following considerations :—

   "*a.* The High Commissioner, as Governor of the Cape Colony, resides at
   Capetown, which is about 700 miles from the northern frontier of the
   Eastern Province, where alone independent native tribes are to be met
   with.

   "*b.* That Natal is surrounded on three sides by territories chiefly occupied by large and powerful independent tribes, with whom the local authorities cannot deal irrespective of the consent of the High Commissioner at Capetown.

"*c.* That in times of disturbance amongst the surrounding communities, the Government of Natal is deprived of that power of timely and effectual action which it might otherwise exercise with great benefit to the interests of peace and civilization.

"*d.* That ever since the annexation of the Orange River Sovereignty (since abandoned) in 1848, the emigrant farmers who settled over the Vaal River, and formed a government of their own, under the style of the South-African Republic, have carried on a system of slavery, under the guise of child-apprenticeship—such children being the result of raids carried on against native tribes, whose men are slaughtered, but whose children and property are seized, the one being enslaved and sold as 'apprentices,' the other being appropriated.

"*e.* That in 1862 this system of slavery was brought to the notice of the High Commissioner and the Secretary of State by Lieutenant-Governer Scott, in the form of a statement made by a Bushman woman named Leya, who had been captured and enslaved by the Boers of the Trans-Vaal Republic, but no steps were then taken to put an end to the practice in question.

"*f.* That on the 25th April, 1865, Lieutenant-Governor Maclean forwarded to the High Commissioner a statement made by Mr. W. Martin, of Maritzburg, dated June 1st, 1865, in which clear and positive evidence, acquired during two visits to the country in 1852 and 1864, was given at length, and in which certain wrongs suffered by the writer, in direct contravention of the treaty entered into between her Majesty's Special Commissioners, Hogge and Owen, in 1852, were set forth.

"*g.* That the existence of this system of slavery, attended as it is by indescribable atrocities and evils, is a notorious fact to all persons acquainted with the Trans-Vaal Republic; that these so-called 'destitute children' are bought and sold under the denomination of 'black ivory;' that these evils were fully admitted by persons officially cognizant of them at a public meeting held in Potchefstroom, the chief town of the Republic, in April, 1868, and that the whole subject has been brought fully under the notice of the High Commissioner.

"*h.* That the following reply was sent to Lieutenant-Governor Maclean, by the High Commissioner:—'I can assure you that I fully sympathize with you in your anxiety to put a stop to what is so strongly described by Mr. Martin, but I am really quite at a loss to discover in what manner I could interfere with any prospect of success. There can scarcely be a doubt that the President, if referred to, would strenuously deny the existence of such traffic. A *bona fide* inquiry would be almost impracticable, and, moreover, it would be beyond the power of the Trans-Vaal Republic, admitting it to have the inclination, to put down a trade which the Boers must find to be very tempting and profitable. Under all the circumstances, I trust that you will, on further consideration, be prepared to acquiesce in my desire to abstain from addressing Mr. Protorius on the subject.'

" *i.* That as a *bona fide* inquiry to be instituted by the Government of the Trans-Vaal Republic would be, under the circumstances, ' quite impracticable,' it is highly important that her Majesty's Government should take other steps to ascertain the truth, and to put a stop to a trade which, however ' tempting and profitable to the Boers,' is a direct breach of the treaty entered into with her Majesty's Commissioners, is an outrage on humanity and civilization, and is an aggravation of the traffic which her Majesty's Government has so long sought to suppress upon the East Coast.

" *j.* That so long as this traffic in children is suffered to exist, there can be little hope for the progress of civilization amongst the native tribes living in the Trans-Vaal Republic, while the prevalence of such practices in the immediate neighbourhood of independent and colonial tribes, has a most pernicious and injurious effect, and tends to lower the position and influence of the whole race.

" *k.* That it is impossible for the High Commissioner, living as he does so far from the scene of these atrocities, to judge clearly and fully of their character and tendencies; but it would be in the power of the Government of Natal, had it the right to act, to interfere in the matter, without entailing any troublesome or costly complications on the Home Government.

" *l.* That the state of peace which the colony of Natal has enjoyed ever since its establishment, combined with the constant recognition here of all the just rights and claims of the natives, have secured for the local government the confidence of the neighbouring independent tribes, and would enable the representatives of her Majesty's authority here, were they freed from the control of the High Commissioner, to exercise a most salutary and beneficent influence over the natives of South-Eastern Africa.

" 2. That a respectful address be presented to the Lieutenant-Governor, forwarding a copy of above resolution; and praying his Excellency to transmit the same to the Right Honourable the Secretary of State for the Colonies for his consideration, together with copies of all documents bearing upon the subject."

It is seldom that resolutions have been passed by a Colonial Assembly surpassing these in the gravity of their statements, or of the issues which they raise. Even those who might be disposed to call in question reports in the newspapers, will be constrained to admit that the deliberate impeachment of the Boers by the Legislative Council of a British colony is a fact which cannot be dismissed with a sneer. Serious charges have been preferred against the Trans-Vaal slaveholders by a body whose right to a voice in the matter cannot be impugned. To these charges no answer has been returned. The Boers maintain a judicious silence; but England has a duty to perform, which, whether they defend themselves, or allow judgment to go by default, she cannot neglect without peril. At all events, it cannot be tolerated, that while a costly squadron is vainly striving to suppress the slave-trade on the East Coast of Africa, the traffic should be allowed to continue unchecked, and without an effort being made to put it down, in a country whose right to enjoy a separate Government is contingent on the fidelity with which it abstains from the practice of slavery and slave-trading.

Of equal importance are the resolutions in favour of the annexation to Natal of the Free State and the Trans-Vaal, which were adopted by the House of Assembly on the 19th of August last. These resolutions declare that a union between the British colonies and the Dutch Republics would be mutually beneficial, and that the dependence of the latter on the Cape Colony and Natal "favours the belief that, sooner or later, they will be "desirous of coming under the dominion of the British Go-"vernment."

The author of this plan of a South African Confederation is really Sir George Grey, who, in a remarkable despatch which was addressed to Sir Edward Lytton, on the 19th November, 1858, elaborated the policy which the Natal Legislature has now revived. The resolutions raise a very large and momentous question—one which cannot be decided superficially or by theoretical considerations, however reasonable. One thing is certain, that a Federal union will not meet with the approval of the statesmen of this country, unless it be self-supporting; and this, therefore, is a point to which its advocates should at once direct their attention. There is good reason to believe that the movement proceeds from within as well as from without; that a powerful party in both Republics are tired of commandos, sick of the ruinous insecurity of their position, alarmed at the moral deterioration of their own race, disgusted with the brutalities of the Boers of the old school. Let, however, the decision on the larger question be what it may, it is impossible that any European community in South Africa can be permitted to build up the institution of slavery in territories which are within the jurisdiction, or subject to the just influence of Great Britain.

I am, my dear Sir, yours very faithfully,

F. W. CHESSON.

LETTER II.

To R. N. FOWLER, Esq. M.P.

MY DEAR SIR,—Two years have elapsed since I addressed my
first Letter to you on the subject of slavery in the Trans-Vaal
Republic, and I regret to state that I have since received an
amount of additional evidence confirming the truth of the statements I then made, which, if published *in extenso*, would swell
this pamphlet into volumes. The numerous letters which I have
received from the Cape and Natal, and from the Dutch territory
itself, fully establish the fact that the old Hollander party
in the Republic is resolutely bent upon enslaving or destroying
the neighbouring tribes, and that it cannot offer to the world
even the sorry excuse that, if its object is successful, it will have
set up civilization in the place of barbarism. It has been too long
assumed that wherever the white man goes he necessarily carries
civilization with him. The time has surely come when this species .
of cant should no longer be allowed to minister to the self-love of
the stronger race, and when Europeans should be made to feel that
they too are barbarians when they practise the vices and crimes
of barbarians.

When, shortly after the assembling of Parliament the year before
last, you brought this subject in an able and temperate speech before
the House of Commons, Mr. Monsell, with characteristic frankness,
admitted the absolute truth of the allegations which you had made,
and reprobated in feeling language the cruel proceedings of the
Boers. "Every statement," he said, "made by the hon. gentle-
"man he was obliged to endorse. Her Majesty's Government had
"not any precisely official information, because we had no diplomatic
"agent in the Trans-Vaal Republic; but at the same time the Govern-
"ment had received, both from the Governor of the Cape and the
"Governor of Natal, and from her Majesty's Commissioner to the
"Mixed Court held at the Cape, statements fully corroborating all
"that had been said by the hon. member." There could be no more

unqualified testimony than that which fell spontaneously from the lips of the Under-Secretary for the Colonies.

I might, indeed, allow our case to rest where it has been placed by Mr. Monsell's emphatic declaration ; but a speech is soon forgotten, and it is necessary that the subject should be recurred to again and yet again, until the fairest territories of South Africa are rescued from the domination of men who, if they are allowed to pursue their evil course without protest or interruption, will assuredly do for South Africa what was done for the North American Continent by those who landed the first cargo of negro slaves on the banks of the James river.

It is satisfactory to know that in reopening this controversy one is now not exclusively dependent on newspaper reports or private sources of information. A Blue Book[*] published in the last session contains the official view of these matters, as well as the lamentable series of statements which ultimately induced the Imperial Government to revoke that odious clause of the treaty with the Boers which permitted the sale of ammunition to them while prohibiting it to the native tribes. The Blue Book opens with a correspondence in which Mr. G. W. Steyn and other inhabitants of the Trans-Vaal Republic make Sir Philip Wodehouse acquainted with details " of " the wholesale slavery that is daily carried on in these remote " regions." Mr. Steyn, in a letter dated Potchefstroom, South " African Republic, 4th December, 1865, says,—

" On the 1st inst. Messrs. Carel Smith and Hayman arrived here from ' Zout-pansberg ' with two loads of young Kaffirs (thirty-one in number), males and females, varying in ages from three to twelve years ; these were publicly disposed of here at from 15l. to 22l. 10s. per head, or, in some instances, exchanged for cattle. . . . . I need not tell your Excellency that it is a matter of serious regret as well as disgust to every civilized inhabitant of the Trans-Vaal that the horrors of slavery are daily increasing here without any prospect of our government taking any measures to prevent it. This way of disposing of Kaffirs is called here ' selling indentureship,' but I could point out several cases where Kaffirs have been kept in the bonds of slavery for more than thirty years. Your Excellency may be a stranger to the fact that we are at present, and are almost every year, at war with several small native tribes near Zoutpansberg. I hesitate not in saying that these annual wars are solely caused by several of our frontier Boers making unprovoked commandos on some Kaffir kraals, shooting the men, and in some instances the women, and capturing the children, which they soon turn over to the profitable account of

[*] Correspondence relating to the alleged Kidnapping and Enslaving of young Africans.

slavery. The following are as near as possible the words spoken to me a few days ago by one of the young Kaffirs who has just been sold, a boy of about twelve years old :—'The Boers shot my father. I was busy milking a buck when one of them took me away. My mother wept bitterly to have a parting look at me, but she was driven away by one of the Boers with a whip.' This is only one of the many instances I could illustrate to prove to your Excellency that whatever the Boers may term it, it is the most unmitigated slavery that is carried on here, and loudly calls for some interference on the part of your Excellency."

A local paper—"De Republikein"—while endeavouring to produce the impression that the government had no desire to encourage the traffic, admitted that the slave trade was "fast becoming " a lucrative branch of commerce," and that " whole waggon-loads " of children are being continually hawked about the country, the " most of which are procured from Zoutpansberg, where several men " have for years past made it a regular trade, most of these children " being bought by them from the natives at low prices, who kidnap, " and often in less merciful manner obtain them from tribes in the " hunting veld; and small parties of natives are even fitted out with " goods and sent down as far as Delagoa bay to traffic for 'black " ivory.' "

For representing to the Governor of the Cape Colony the existence of this state of things, Mr. Steyn was threatened with a trial for high treason, and indeed President Pretorius told him that " it was high time he was banished from the country for cor- " responding with foreign powers about political matters." As the Convention, by virtue of which the Republic enjoys its independence, forbids the practice of slavery, the matter was assuredly one with regard to which it was highly important that the High Commissioner should receive accurate information ; and Mr. Steyn, in calling his Excellency's attention to the infraction of the treaty, discharged a duty to the Republic no less than to the cause of human freedom. To do him justice, he was not at all intimidated by the vapourings of Mr. Pretorius, or by the prosecution with which he was threatened at the hands of the state attorney. He was, moreover, supported by several citizens of Potchefstroom as humane and courageous as himself. Both the Rev. J. Ludorf and the Rev. G. T. Jeffreys deposed to the fact that black children had been offered for sale in the streets of Potchefstroom, and that they were eye-witnesses of one of these transactions. " We could not learn," says Mr. Jeffreys, " how these children had become ' orphans,' or under what circum-

" stances they had been taken to the kantoor at Schomansdal. Under
" the waggon were three or four Kaffir children which he (the owner)
" represented as *his property*. On looking about the erf adjacent we
" found, behind a pile of dried thatch which hid them from the road
" the children themselves, nineteen in number, varying in age from
" seven to eleven years. They were naturally very shy, but one or
" two of them, in answer to questions put by Mr. Ludorf, who
" spoke to them in their own language, gave us to understand that
" their fathers had been shot down at their kraals—whether by white
" or by coloured people I did not learn—and that they had been
" forcibly torn away from their mothers. This may have applied,
" however, only to *some* of them, not to *all*." " Inboeking," or so-
called apprenticeship, is recognized by the Law of the Republic;
but although that law is wide enough to admit every kind of abuse,
it was in this instance technically violated. Mr. Pretorius therefore made a show of doing something. He fulminated a proclamation against the slave trade, recited the article of the Constitution
prohibiting it, and ordered the Landdrosts to investigate all cases
of slave dealing which might be brought before them.

Sir Philip Wodehouse responded to Mr. Steyn's appeal by
addressing a despatch to the President, in which he called his
attention " to the public sale at Potchefstroom and its vicinity of
" native children under circumstances which warrant a belief that
" they came into the possession of the dealers by means of the
" murder of their parents," and demanded the punishment of the
criminals. This requisition Mr. Pretorius promised to comply with.
Such acts, he assured his Excellency, would not be allowed to pass
unpunished. But there was one demand in Sir Philip's letter
which the President entirely passed over. His Excellency
said,—

" I cannot close this communication without inviting your most serious and
immediate attention to those provisions of the laws of the South African
Republic under which, as I am informed, native children and youths, called
orphans, or perhaps made so by the murder of their parents, can be registered
as apprentices for a term of twenty-one years, and can, during that term, be sold
from hand to hand as a marketable commodity. I must plainly state that such
arrangements, no matter under what name they may be disguised, can only be
regarded as sanctioning practical slavery, and as being therefore a clear violation of one of the most important stipulations of the Convention between the
government and that of her Majesty. It is my duty, therefore, to seek, at the
hands of your government, a plain and positive repeal of any such laws, and
the enactment of such penalties as will effectually put a stop to any further

traffic in human beings, and will satisfy her Majesty's Government that the terms of the Convention will be honourably adhered to."

This was going to the very root of the question. Of what avail was the punishment of one or two miserable wretches who had only just exceeded the limits of the law, while the law itself afforded every possible facility for the kidnapping and enslaving of children, so long as they were declared to be orphans and made to pass through a form of apprenticeship. It is not surprising that Mr. Pretorius should have endeavoured to evade the question which was addressed to him ; and that, although the Governor renewed his demand, he failed to obtain that satisfaction to which, as the representative of Great Britain, he was entitled. As the sequel showed, " the assurances " in which the President dealt so largely were not worth the paper on which they were written ; while Sir Philip Wodehouse, instead of insisting that vague promises should be followed by acts which would prove the good faith of the authorities, abruptly closed the discussion.

The Governor's correspondence on the subject with the Home Government was re-opened by his Excellency on June 3rd, 1868, who then enclosed two letters " describing the cruelties practised " by the people of the Trans-Vaal Republic on the native tribes in " their neighbourhood, and the systematic reduction of their mem- " bers to a state of slavery." These letters are not printed, lest their publication should compromise the writers ; but his Excellency plainly hinted that, in his judgment, the time had arrived when the policy of continuing to supply the Boers with ammunition to be used against the natives should be abandoned; and on the 24th November following the Duke of Buckingham gave him authority to act upon his views—an authority which, if it had been granted two years earlier, might have prevented much bloodshed, and would, at all events, have saved this country from the stigma of furnishing material aid to a cause which it knew to be an unrighteous one.

In my former Letter I adverted to the extraordinary proclamation which the Trans-Vaal President issued after the discovery of the gold-fields in the country of Moselekatse, and which, in the words of Sir Philip Wodehouse, " carries the boundaries of that State on " the west about half way to the Atlantic, including the gold-fields " and assuming the complete control of all the trade between this

" colony and the tribes in the interior, and on the east claims
" access to the sea in Delagoa Bay." In the interior, as the Rev.
John McKenzie has pointed out, the grasping Boers pretended
that not only were the southern gold-fields within their boundary,
but that so were " Lechulathebe at Lake N'Gami, Macheng, Sechele,
" Mosreleele, Mokhosi, Mangope, Gasiitsirve, Montsiive, Maikeewe,
" Makobe, Mahura, Jantje, and the chiefs at and near Kuruman,
" and more than a dozen native chiefs who have never owed
" allegiance to the Boers ;" while they actually claimed the southern
portion of Delagoa Bay, which was ceded by the chiefs of the
country to Captain Owen in the year 1825, and which is recognized
as English territory in a treaty between Great Britain and
Portugal. Mr. Pretorius, when asked for an explanation, made
no attempt to justify his indecent act of aggression. His motive
undoubtedly was a desire both to command the whole trade of the
interior and to open up a route to the sea which should be independent of British territory. Of course so far as we were concerned he gained nothing by his paper annexation, for the British
Government at once asserted its rights over the southern half of
Delagoa Bay. Since then he has been negotiating with the
Portuguese for a port at the mouth of the Usutu. If the Trans-
Vaal people confined themselves to legitimate commerce, we might
sympathize with their efforts to obtain an outlet; but so long as
they practise kidnapping, and the East African slave-trade is carried
on, so long will it be a public calamity if the Boers should gain a
footing on the coast.

Mr. Viljoen was the envoy chosen by the Trans-Vaal Government to negotiate for the cession of the gold-fields in the territory
of Macheng, the Chief of the Bamangwato. Jan Viljoen had endeavoured, but in vain, to persuade Macheng to make a present of the
gold-fields to the Boers. The chief, who knew well the kind of
people the Boers are, refused, and was persistent in his refusal.
What effect his obstinacy had upon the mind of the Dutch
emissary Mr. Viljoen himself has confessed with singular ingenuous-
ness. Here is a letter which he wrote on the occasion :—

[Translation.]

" *Macheng's Town.*

"THE WORTHY AND BELOVED NEPHEW, J. LEE,

"I cannot neglect again to write a few lines to you, my worthy friend.
We have got to this place in good health through the goodness of our Lord,
hoping that these few lines may find you and your family in good health.

Worthy Jonnie, as to news there is little. I had yesterday a great dispute with Macheng. It is so as we had heard. Macheng says that Selkaats (Moselekatse) has no country here; that it is his country where Moselekatse lives. Please to say all this to Moselekatse. Worthy Jonnie, I trust it all to you. If you can manage it, set the fire on the vagabonds (vagebonden), if you can manage it. This is not an opportunity for writing all to you. I will write circumstantially by another opportunity. Be greeted by us all, &c.

"J. W. VILJOEN, Sen."

This letter illustrates the religious hypocrisy with which the Boers garnish even their worst deeds. This man is "in good "health through the goodness of our Lord;" but yet in the same breath he says, "If you can manage it, set the fire on the vaga- "bonds," the sole offence which "the vagabonds" had committed being their determination to keep their own country out of the clutches of the freebooters, and their desire to become British subjects.

The history of this letter is thus told by Mr. McKenzie, the London Society's missionary :—

"This letter was never sealed, was read by those to whom Viljoen confided it, was afterwards handed over to Macheng, and so never reached its destination. It is surely a very disgraceful production as coming from a public officer of a 'Christian' government. Had it succeeded in its object, the lives of the missionary and his family, the lives of some twelve Englishmen trading in Macheng's Town, some of them married, would have been placed in the utmost danger, not to mention the Bamangwato whom Viljoen devoted to the 'fire' of the savage Matebele, because their chief had sought the protection of the British Government. Macheng's Town is an important centre for the trade of the interior. English goods to the colonial value of many thousand pounds are there exposed for sale; and on all this Viljoen sought to bring destruction. I send you the above as an item of news, but should your Excellency desiderate a formal complaint from British subjects against this letter, what I have now written may be regarded as such, and as written in behalf of myself and family, of the Englishmen, hunters, traders, and gold-diggers in Macheng's Town and country, and also in behalf of the Bamangwato who are thus betrayed on account of their partiality for the English. There is no doubt that the letter in Macheng's possession is genuine. Several Boer hunters have already testified to this, and I myself recognize it as his handwriting."

But the recent achievements of the Boers in the interior do not end with this episode in the diplomatic career of Herr Viljoen. On the 28th of August, 1868, Montsioa Taoane, Chief of the Baralong, writes to Governor Wodehouse that, although his people has treated the Boers, when they were suffering great hardships, with the utmost kindness and hospitality, and had subsequently assisted them to defeat Mosclekatse and the warlike Matabele, they had yet in return suffered the grossest injustice at the hands of their quondam allies. But let the chief speak for himself:—

"In 1853 by the most crying injustice the Boers attacked us, and after fighting a whole day they found out that '*there existed no grounds whatever for such bloodshed;*' calling themselves '*the blind commando,*' they left. All the farmers of Mariko then fled, fearing we would retaliate. Several seasons passed, till at last the Boers made some overtures for a settlement. On coming to terms with Commandant Jan Viljoen and President M. Pretorius, the old boundary-lines were agreed to on both sides. But, knowing how little the promises of the Boers could be trusted, we would not go back to our old residence Lotlakana, but continued to sojourn with the Bangoaketsi tribe, to keep somewhat out of the Boers' reach.

"And now, without the least provocation on our side (though the Boers have from time to time murdered some of my people and enslaved several small villages of our Balala), the Trans-Vaal Republic deprive us by the said proclamation of our lands and liberty, against which we would protest in the strongest terms, and entreat your Excellency, as her Britannic Majesty's High Commissioner, to protect us."

Comment on the ingratitude, as well as the immorality of these proceedings, is unnecessary; but, lest the reader should still be tempted to imagine that the Boers may perhaps, after all, carry some kind of civilization into the interior, let him read the following extract from the letter of a German missionary which Governor Wodehouse sent to the Secretary of State for the Colonies:—

"You will be surprised to hear that we have a visit of Trans-Vaal Boers. We do not believe them to be only elephant-hunters, but also slave-traders. They have bought many children at Ngamisca and elsewhere, whereof they make no secret. They give a (paviaanhout) rifle, therefore from 2*l.* or 3*l.*, for each child. If it will come to the knowledge of the Herero, then the bane of the slave-trade will have come also over this land, and principally the poor Berg Damra will have to suffer under it. But no doubt the Herero will sell also the children of the poor of their own nation, of which there are thousands living in the open field."

Thus far the Governor of the Cape Colony. If, however, we turn to the despatches of Mr. Keate, the Lieutenant-Governor of Natal, we find a repetition of the same kind of testimony. So greatly had the Boers alarmed the natives, that tribes dwelling many days' journey in the interior have sent embassies to Natal, to implore the protection of the British Government. No higher tribute could be paid to the prestige of this country in South

Africa, or to the success with which the Colony of Natal has managed its own native affairs. The reputation of Mr. Shepstone appears to have gone forth to these distant tribes as that of a man whose inflexible love of justice may be relied upon in every emergency. The embassies from the Amandebele, the Amaswazi, and the Umzila tribes have not been sufficiently appreciated in this country; but in reality they form a bright chapter in the history of South Africa. Natal has never been afflicted with a native war. Since the British flag has waved there it has proved the synonym of peace and justice. The colonists have never sought to reap where others sow, and the natives have been treated as men, not as vermin. Yet more than 200,000 of them reside in the colony, thus outnumbering the handful of English people in the proportion of ten or twelve to one. They make good servants and industrious labourers, contribute their quota towards the taxes, and are a source of strength, instead of weakness, to the community. It might be thought that even the Boer would learn the lesson which the example of Natal teaches; but he unfortunately closes his ears and shuts his eyes to all experience by which he might profit : in a word, he is unteachable.

This is the statement of Ntekwane, alias Jonas Zililo Mushwan, and Makulimela, messengers from the Chief Malamlcla Nonkupuna Langa, of the Amandebele tribe, residing on the river Umhalagweni, a tributary of the Limpopo Oori Ululi or Bembe river, the Ubemba of the Zulus :—

"Our chief rules over many people of different languages and habits, and over a large extent of country, on both banks of the Limpopo river; he and the majority of his people belong to the Zulu race and speak the Zulu language; and he has occupied the country he rules over for many generations, his father Bolile, and his grandfather Umbiluna, and their ancestors, were born in it. Every chief takes the name of Langa, although it is necessary he should have his distinctive name as well.

"Langa's country produces grain of different kinds in great abundance, cattle, sheep, and goats, four metals, one of which is iron, and another copper, the other two are white metals, one of which is like that used for bullets, but whiter, and the other whiter still and harder. The country abounds also in game of all descriptions, such as the elephant, rhinoceros, giraffe, sea-cow, lion, buffalo, eland, hartebeeste, gnu, blesbok, and many others, such as the impala and water-bok; it contains every thing necessary to make its inhabitants happy, and it is besides very healthy; but our chief says, ' What are all these, if peace cannot be had, and if the people are not sure that their children will be left to them ? ' His people live four days' walk west of Zoutpansberg, the Boers are their neighbours, but not close, and they are always finding some excuse for exacting tribute and carrying off their children into slavery; they shoot the parents and take the children, and the children are never heard of again. The fear of the Boers has caused all the people to abandon the level country, and it is a common practice for the Boers to make raids during the planting season and carry off all the children they find with their parents in the fields, shooting all those who are too old to forget their homes; they have several times tried to get possession of the person of our chief, to put him to death, as they have other chiefs, or to extort ransom from his people. Langa is afraid of them, and will not meet them. He was once in their power, and was not released until his people gave them one hundred guns, thirty elephants' tusks, and a large number of cattle, and this was justified by no charge whatsoever against him; they invited him to go and see them, and on his complying such was the treatment he received. They have also encouraged one of his sons, named Masibi, to rebel against his father, and hope by means of this young man to destroy him and scatter his people as dogs among them to work for them. Langa has been specially careful to avoid giving any cause of offence: he allows hunting parties of Boers to pass through his country unmolested, and when they lose their oxen has them taken back to them.

"Lately another chief, named Umgombana, was compelled by war with the Boers to abandon his country: he with his people took refuge with Langa, and brought with them waggons and horses which they had captured from the Boers. Langa immediately restored to the Boers all the property he could collect which had been captured from them, so as to avoid offending them; but he hears that they intend to take measures against him. Langa will defend himself, but he says he is tired of war, and of rearing children to be taken by others."

Perhaps the most touching part of the statement is that which I have yet to quote. The chief says that "he cannot send "elephants' tusks, or any thing bulky, to show his sincerity, because "the Boers would not permit the passage of any such present, if "they knew it was for the English Government;" but he, however, sends "a few feathers," which his messengers were able to conceal. Could any thing more conclusively prove the existence of the reign of terror which the Boers have established in the interior?

Mr. Keate, in a very interesting despatch, dated the 24th September, 1868, makes some suggestive remarks on the evil influence which is exerted by the European slave-traders upon the native tribes. He says, "It is very much to be feared, however, "that owing to the example set by the Portuguese for so long a "time past, and to the later practice of some of the subjects of the "Trans-Vaal Government, all these tribes, or nearly all, with the "marked exception of the Zulus, pursue a policy which is favour- "able to the prosecution of the slave-trade. Captives taken in war, "children, or adults, are valuable property. The slave-ships take "the adults because, when carried beyond the seas, they cannot by

D

" absconding return to their homes. The subjects of the Trans-
" Vaal take the children, because their infancy renders their ever
" reaching their homes hopeless. This slavery in the Trans-Vaal
" territory, on the native soil of the slave, gives rise to the most
" atrocious crimes. It requires and leads to the extermination of
" the parents and friends whenever possible of the captured children,
" who otherwise might be sought for and be inveigled away. It
" makes desirable, too, for its purposes the annihilation of the very
" commonest instincts of human nature."

If Sir T. F. Buxton were in the House of Commons he could
now present the question of the East African slave-trade in a new
aspect. Portugal may abolish that nefarious trade, and new
treaties with the Sultan of Zanzibar may mitigate its horrors, and
contract the area in which it is carried on, but there will be little
hope of its entire suppression so long as the Boers employ their
influence in the interior to bolster up the traffic in human flesh.

But the official evidence does not close with the despatches of
Governor Keate. In 1868 Mr. E. L. Layard, of the Mixed Commission Court, Cape Town, called Lord Stanley's attention to the
subject. After epitomizing the facts which had been submitted to
him by the inhabitants of the Trans-Vaal territory, he says, " I fear
" from the records of former transactions that Mr. —— is right in
" saying that unless a Commission is sent to investigate the subject
" on the spot, no information will be got from the authorities, as
" witness the conduct of the officials sent by the Free State, osten-
" sibly for the purpose of aiding the British Commissioner to in-
" vestigate the charges preferred in 1855 (see Despatch from Mr.
" Surtees, No. 15, of December 3, 1855). These very men purchased
" children while on their mission, and threw every impediment in
" the way of the truth being ascertained."

It is not surprising that Boers from the Orange Free State—a
Republic which has not scrupled to despoil the Basutos and other
tribes of many thousands of square miles of fertile territory—should
have been unable to resist the temptation to lay felonious hands
upon Kaffir children ; but it is well that the fact should be put on
record by British officials so justly esteemed as are Mr. Surtees
and Mr. Layard.

Mr. Layard forwarded to Lord Stanley a copy of a letter
which had been addressed to the Hon. R. Godlonton by a Mr.
M. S. Fitzgerald, on his return from " a most wretched and

miserable existence" of five years' duration in the Trans-Vaal country. He says,—

"The scenes of cruelty and crime, blood and murder, that I have "witnessed are beyond the power of words to delineate; *friendly* "*and helpless, unarmed and unprotected* natives massacred in cold "blood, and without the slightest provocation, their misfortune being "that they possessed that which excited the cupidity and avarice of "those white savages, whose very nature and thirst for rapine and "plunder far exceeded any excesses ever committed by their "sable brethren. Yes; they possessed cattle, produce, *and children.*"

He then goes on to mention the names of office-holders in the Republic who do not scruple to profit by these odious crimes—of one especially who, on obtaining leave of absence, accompanied a band of marauders who were absent two months, and then returned "with their ill-gotten spoil and a large number of native children." "Even ministers of religion," he says, "do not scruple or disdain "to sully their cloth with the odious traffic."

Your motion for the publication of papers had the effect of inducing Mr. Pratt, the Consul of the Trans-Vaal Republic in London, to address a letter to Lord Clarendon, in which he requested his Lordship to include in the official correspondence the following extract from the proceedings of the Volksraad on March 16th, 1866:—

"The report from the Commission for examining the law against slavery was read and adopted on the ground that the people of the South African Republic wish strictly to adhere to the terms of the Convention of January 16th, 1852, between her Majesty's Commissioners and the emigrant Boers, in order to avoid slavery:—

"Art. 1. It is determined that all persons having destitute orphan children shall in future be looked upon as their guardians, and be held responsible as such to the Government who are co-guardians. The government shall strictly see that no further registration or transfer of children shall take place, save and except through the death of their guardian, in which case the widow or next of kin shall be held responsible for their guardianship. If there are no next of kin, then the government shall appoint another guardian, the government still remaining the co-guardians.

"Art. 2. All destitute native orphan children shall be looked after, and brought up, and be well treated according to law.

"Art. 3. All officers and officials are strictly ordered to uphold and enforce the law as narrowly as possible whereby it is forbidden that any hunter, trader, or person whatsoever shall bring into the Republic any Kaffir children, *unless the same can be proved to be orphan and destitute* (as in Art. 2).

"Art. 4. Whenever any official or officer is careless, or shall neglect to enforce the law in this respect, he shall be punished by a fine of 2000 dollars, or, in default, be committed to prison for the term of two years.

"Art. 5. Parties acting against or breaking the law to be punished by a fine of 500*l.*, or, in default, five years' imprisonment with hard labour.

"Any official acting in collusion with the chief offender in breaking the law shall be punished equally with the said offender."

What did the Consul for the South African Republic hope to accomplish by the production of this law? Nobody supposes that any but orphan and destitute children are held in servitude ; the contention being that they are made orphan and destitute by Dutch bullets. The Foreign Secretary saw this, for Mr. Otway, in reply, states that Lord Clarendon would be glad if Mr. Pratt "could inform him how it comes to pass that there are so many " 'destitute native orphan children' in the territories of the Republic ": as to require legislation on their behalf by the authorities, and also " how the citizens of the Republic came to be possessed of them." Mr. Pratt, however, does not answer this question. Commandos, he says, have generally been organized "to repress frequent depre- " dations committed on the cattle by the blacks ; and the Boers are " so strongly opposed to these commandos, that in a recent session " of the Volksraad a resolution was passed to entirely discontinue " them." He also says,—

"I do not deny that isolated cases of ill-treatment may have occurred in out- lying districts, or that the Boers in the early days of trekking, with their wives and families, may have been driven to hostile measures in order to protect themselves from constant attacks of natives, particularly as they had no stand- ing army of their own ; but with reference to charges reflecting discredit on the government and people alike, such as obtaining 6000 children annually, and the burning of children alive, I have every reason to believe that the former will, on investigation in the Republic, prove to be a gross exaggeration, and the latter if it occurred at all, was not the act of the Boers, but of the Kaffirs themselves against Kaffirs. The chief seat of native disturbances has been at Zoutpansberg, and these appear to have been caused by Kaffir superintendents, who, it would seem, have fostered ill-feeling between the native tribes, in consequence of which they have lately been exposed and dismissed."

Let the Boers have the benefit of this defence, and what then? Nobody alleges that the commandos are ostensibly despatched on kidnapping expeditions; but the charge is, that the commandos, after killing the men, capture the women and children, and make slaves of them. This Mr. Pratt does not deny ; but he falls back on the plea of "exaggeration," as if a thousand witnesses, com- prising the best men of the Republic and of the two British colonies, had all conspired, for some mysterious purpose, to paint the Boers in colours blacker than the night.

When Mr. Pratt wrote his letter he could not have heard of the women who, a few months previously, had been publicly flogged at Rustenburg. The details were published in the Cape and Natal papers. They had deserted from the service of their master because, as they told the Landdrost, " he would not permit them to attend the " mission school." If any thing in this world marks the lowest stage of barbarism, it is the maltreatment of women physically incapable of defending themselves. The flogging of these unhappy Kaffir girls inflicts a stain on the Boers which all the waters of the Atlantic could not wash out. Nor was it an exceptional atrocity ; for a correspondent of my own, who writes from the Trans-Vaal, informs me that " woman-flogging in public is by no means an " extraordinary occurrence in that country."

Mr. Pratt, moreover, surely could not have read the report of the Commission of Inquiry from which I quoted in my first letter. It will be seen from that document that the cases of ill-treatment are by no means " isolated," and that, whatever may have been done in " the early days of trekking," these cases form part of the history of the present time. In no respect is it in my power to soften the picture which I have already presented to the public ; its darkest features being amply borne out by official evidence.

When Mr. Pratt addressed his letter to Lord Clarendon he could not have known that in the district of Utrecht the Dutch exchange dogs for children. No portion of my previous statement has excited greater indignation than this ; yet it has since been confirmed by perfectly independent evidence. The Rev. P. Huet, a Dutch clergyman, who formerly resided in the Republic, declares that children are bartered for dogs, or even for objects of less value[7] ; and in the last letter I received from the lamented Mr. William Martin, of Natal, who sacrificed his valuable life in the cause of philanthropy, he says, " It is only fair " to say that I now know—being in the vicinity of the Amas-" wazi country—that some of that tribe wickedly sell their " children to the Boers for dogs." His comment on this is that " the Boers are not to blame for all the slavery in the Trans-

[7] Het lot der zwarten in Transvaal mededeelingen omtrent de slavernij en Wreedheden in de Zuid.—" Afrikaansche Republiek." Door P. Huet. Utrecht (Holland). 1869.

" Vaal, and that there are therefore two sides to every question."
I am quite willing to give them the benefit of this qualification.
They may be no worse than the ruffians who sell children for
dogs; but can any one pretend that they are better? It is difficult even thus to divide the blame; for these heathen know
nothing of that religion of justice and charity which the Boer
professes to regard as the law of his life.

But Mr. Pratt appeals to the laws passed by the Volksraad.
Mr. Huet's testimony on this subject is entirely to the point:—

" 'One will ask,' he says, ' Whether there are no laws to prevent ill-treatment and to guarantee liberty to the poor captives, at least after some time of
servitude?' Certainly, with a truly hypocritical philanthropy, certain laws
are made, for instance, that, in case of transgression, the master has to bring
his servant to the field-cornet to have him punished; but the master cares
little for the law, and the field-cornet just as little, and the servant does not even
know the existence of the law.

" The same is true of the apprenticeship. Till their twenty-second, or in
some places till their twenty-fifth year, they are apprenticed. All this time they
have to serve without payment. The Boers say, ' This is right, because we
want compensation for the expense and trouble spent in their education.'
Expense and trouble and education! As soon as the poor creatures are able
to walk they have to look after the cattle, or to carry the youngest child of the
mistress, which is often as big and twice as heavy as themselves. Till the
twenty-second or twenty-fifth year! And all this time without any reward,
but perhaps a thoroughly worn-out piece of clothing, invectives, curses, whip-
pings! And when the time of servitude is over, are they then free? Who
will give them freedom? Who will make them acquainted with the law?
Nobody. It is slavery in the fullest sense of the word—with this exception,
that slave states have their laws and overseers, who at least keep the ill-
treatment within certain limits; whilst here nobody, I say nobody, cares for
their lot, and they are thoroughly given over to the caprice of their cruel
masters and often yet more cruel mistresses.

" When the servant maid becomes marriageable the master's permission
must be obtained for her taking a husband, which permission it is unnecessary
to say is in most cases refused, and, if granted, the applicant must pay for the
girl either with money or with work.

" After all this let nobody say that slavery or the slave-trade is abolished in
any part of the Trans-Vaal Republic, as has been stated by some newspapers."

The truth is that laws become a simple mockery and pretence
if a government is unable or unwilling to enforce them; or if
there be not a public opinion just and powerful enough to com-
pel their execution. The laws of the Trans-Vaal, so far as they
are supposed to discourage slavery, or to mitigate the evils of the
system, have been, and are intended to be, a dead letter. They

were made to throw dust in the eyes of a British Governor, to hoodwink the British Government, to be quoted in Europe as a proof that the Boers are a civilized people, who may be trusted with even more power and more territory than they have yet obtained.

These people deserve to be pitied as well as condemned. Trained in the school of slaveholding they migrated into the wilderness at a time when the right of the strong to enslave the weak was still widely recognized as the law of nature. They had been taught that slavery was the normal condition of the black man; that the curse which was pronounced upon Ham justified the perpetual enslavement of every dusky tribe which inhabited the African continent; and that, in the order of Providence, Kaffirs and Hottentots, and every mixed and intermediate race, were destined to share the fate of the negroes who toiled in Carolina rice-swamps and on Cuban sugar-plantations. In passing judgment upon them it therefore becomes us to temper justice with mercy. They have suffered the penalty which always follows the evil-doer—a penalty which no community that violates the moral law can escape. Their fertile country is undeveloped, because freemen will not till the land which slaves water with their tears; it is impoverished, because the blight of war is more deadly than any pestilence; it is torn by miserable factions, because it is impossible that order can be maintained in a country where law is despised. The words which Schiller puts into the mouth of Wallenstein are pregnant with truth—

> "Who sows the serpent's teeth, let him not hope
> To reap a joyous harvest. Every crime
> Has, in the moment of its perpetration,
> Its own avenging angel."

I cannot believe that the Imperial Government will, by adopting craven councils, abandon its duty in this matter—a duty which it owes no less to the Boers, and to our own countrymen whose fate is bound up with theirs, than to the native tribes of South Africa. If we had shown more forbearance towards them, even in Sir Harry Smith's time, perhaps they might have withdrawn from their evil path. It is, however, foolish to indulge in vain regrets over the past when we may yet control the future. That future we cannot but regard with dismay if we permit the establishment of a new slave-state in the interior of South Africa.

I feel confident that your best efforts, and those of the other members of the Society in the House of Commons, will be exerted to prevent this great calamity.

I remain,

Yours very faithfully,

F. W. CHESSON.

LETTER III.

To CHARLES BUXTON, Esq., M.P.

MY DEAR SIR,—I ask permission to address these concluding observations to you, because you have manifested a deep interest in one of the questions upon which it is my intention to touch, and because, moreover, I am sure that you will be disposed to take a large view of our responsibilities in South Africa.

In the two preceding letters I have dealt mainly with the question of slavery in the Trans-Vaal Republic; but incidentally I have made repeated allusions to the affairs of the Orange Free State. This Dutch Republic, like its neighbour, is bound hand and foot to the old Hollander party. Seventeen years ago, although it was then inhabited by a population the majority of whom were loyal to the Crown, it ceased to be a British possession. The late Sir George Clerk, her Majesty's Special Commissioner, was the agent employed to carry out the policy of Downing Street. He at first veiled his ulterior designs, but it soon appeared that he was sent out expressly to accomplish the separation of the Orange River Sovereignty from our South African territories. As it was necessary that his policy should be supported by a show of popular consent, he was instructed to go through the farce of appearing to consult the people; and therefore we find him holding private, not public, meetings of the inhabitants, and even getting his proposals adopted by a so-called Assembly of Delegates. It is, however, a fact that the only delegates who were elected by the people refused to be a party to his scheme for the dismemberment of the empire, and that, in consequence, he practically ignored their existence as a representative body. He found it convenient to recognize as delegates a number of persons who had been always hostile to British rule; and with them he concluded the Convention which secures to the Free State such title to the enjoyment of its independence as it can be said to possess. " The Committee of Delegates," who were chosen by the people, declare in their protest (dated 17th February, 1854), that " Sir George Clerk entered " into negotiations with these persons (the self-elected delegates), " with the view of resigning the Government of this portion of " her Majesty's dominions into their hands, or to a government " about to be formed by them, and refused to acknowledge or " treat with us, the lawfully-elected representatives of the people, " without even deigning to give any public notice of his intention " to ignore us, or recognize others as such." Although large public meetings were held in the principal towns of the Sovereignty, and in those of the Cape Colony, to protest against the Convention, the Commissioner would not even give time for a reference to England. His instructions, no doubt, were very imperative, and he fulfilled them to the letter. All the evidence on this subject combines to establish the truth of the serious allegations made in the memorial presented by the Cape merchants in London to the Duke of Buckingham in August 1868. The memorialists, who were headed by Mr. George Thompson and other well-known ex-colonists, allege that "the abandonment of the " Sovereignty was effected in opposition to the declared opinions " of all the English residents, and of by far the largest and most " influential residents of all other races; it was earnestly remon- " strated against by all classes of the Cape Colonists; it was in " despite of the urgent entreaties of the surrounding native " chiefs, even those with whom we had been recently at war; " and in stern opposition to the opinion and advice of every " missionary who resided in the country or knew any thing of " its affairs."

Nor can it be argued that these remonstrances were not justified by subsequent events. When a weak government was substituted for a strong one; when "rebels," for whose capture large rewards had been offered, suddenly found that rebellion was at least profitable to them; when the old Dutch party, whose path in the interior had been stained with violence and blood, discovered that the only obstacle to their aggressions was at last removed, it was impossible that the Free State could enter upon a career of peaceful prosperity. Every one of the conditions necessary to ensure such a future were wholly wanting.

Next to the English, the most powerful neighbours of the Free State Boers are the Basutos, who once occupied a considerable part of the Orange River Sovereignty, but have been driven eastwards by successive waves of colonization. At a remote period the ancestors of this tribe swept down from the north—in fact they derive their name from the Lesuto river, which flows into the Indian Ocean not far from Delagoa Bay. Until my friends, MM. Casalis (of the Paris Evangelical Missionary Society) and Arbousset visited Basutoland in 1833, that country was a *terra incognita*. The fame of the French missionaries had reached Moshesh, the paramount chief of the Basutos, and, through some Griqua hunters, he invited them to visit Thaba Bosigo—his capital—and to establish missions among his people. They accepted his invitation, and the result will not surprise those who are acquainted with the practical wisdom, as well as the disinterested zeal, of these missionaries. They taught the natives habits of industry by personal example. They not only weaned them from cannibalism, but so completely stamped out that barbarous custom, that only the memory of it was left in the land. Christianity made many converts, whilst those who still clung to idolatry were yet induced to acquire some of the blessings of education, and to become industrious graziers and farmers. Mr. Chapman, the African traveller, remarks that " the strength of " the Mission lies in the schools. The natives, though they may " not care for Christianity, have great respect for, to them, the " wonderful arts of reading and writing. They send their chil- " dren to the mission schools to learn these accomplishments. " The books used there have been written by Europeans, and " convey European ideas. The minds of the youthful savages " are thus introduced to civilized thoughts, feelings, and customs, " and in this way the missionaries are laying the foundation of " future civilization." Moshesh himself learnt to read in a Sunday School. Two of his sons were educated at Cape Town under the direction of Sir George Grey ; and one of them, who speaks English tolerably well and French fluently, is now shut up in Paris, where he is fighting for the land of his adoption.

Many years ago a third son, who had been sent here for his education, died at Canterbury.

It might have been thought that the spectacle of an uncivilized tribe, gradually but surely emerging from the darkness of its normal condition, would have created a feeling of sympathy on the part even of the Boers. It might have been thought that they would have regarded the elevation of this native race as affording a ground of hope for the future security of their own borders, and as a pledge that civilized white men were not for ever to live in immediate contact with a mass of irreclaimable barbarism. Unfortunately, however, the Basutos were offensive to the Boers, not merely because they were black men whose intelligence rendered them more eager to defend their rights, but also because they lived in what has been called " the garden of Africa." This, in the eyes of their covetous neighbours, was " the head and " front of their offending ;" and until they had been forced to give up their pleasant corn-fields and orchards to the west of the Caledon river, there could be no peace between them and the Boers.

When people are determined to commit aggression, a pretext is never wanting. The pretext in South Africa was, that the Basutos were cattle-stealers. How to preserve law and order on remote frontiers is one of those difficult problems which even Indian administrators have been unable effectually to solve. Cattle-stealing is an offence which ought to be repressed and punished, but in a country where the frontier is an extensive one, and cattle are very numerous, detection of the thieves is peculiarly difficult. If it were necessary, one might fairly argue that a people who had repeatedly plundered the Basutos of land had no right to complain if, in return, the Basutos stole their cattle. But what if both parties are cattle-stealers ? Surely no hypocrisy can be baser than that which prompts one man to affect indignation at the misconduct of another who is not more culpable than himself. Yet if we may accept the authority of Sir Philip Wodehouse, this is the position in which the Boers are placed. The late Governor of the Cape Colony, writing to the President of the Free State on the 21st of May, 1868, says, " It will probably " be within your knowledge that about the year 1861 the Go- " vernment of the Free State agreed, in concert with Moshesh, to " appoint a joint Commission to inquire into the border robberies. " That Commission, I believe, reported to your government,

" that, so far as the district of Smithfield was concerned, the " thefts of stock from the Basutos very far exceeded those which " they had committed on subjects of the Free State." The Boers and the Basutos having both stolen cattle, what difference is there between them ? I know of none, except that, to quote a line from Hannah More, the latter "stand convicted of a darker skin."

The war between the Orange Free State and the Basutos was concluded by the intervention of the British Government, who received Moshesh and his tribe as British subjects, and then signed a Convention with the Boers, by which they were placed in possession of the very territory concerning which Sir Philip Wodehouse had said that the cession of it "would deprive the tribe of a great portion of "the land best suited to them, " and would coop them up in comparatively barren tracts." The Basutos being British subjects at the time it may well be doubted whether the ignoble plea of " necessity" justified a British Governor in being a party to this extensive con. fiscation of their land; and it is equally doubtful whether the destruction or abandonment of four of the French Missionary stations which has resulted from the convention of North Aliwal can be said to redound to the honour of the British name. The Rev. F. Daumas, the senior missionary in Basutoland, and a man to whose energy and zeal Sir Philip Wodehouse him-self has paid a high tribute, came to England, as you know, in the hope that the Colonial Office would rescue his mission and the Basuto people from spoliation ; but his efforts, as well as our own [a], unfortunately failed to modify a policy which, while it entailed grievous losses on our native allies and on the enlight-ened men who had promoted the cause of peace and civilization amongst them, rewarded the aggressive Boers with the spoils of an unhallowed victory.

The attempt which has been recently made by the Trans-Vaal Republic, and more especially by the Orange Free State, to esta-blish their jurisdiction over a portion of the territories of the Griqua chief Waterboer is a yet more recent illustration of the aggressive tendency of the Dutch governments. These territories include the most valuable of the diamond-fields, and therefore the

[a] Mr. Charles Gilpin and Mr. Fowler also brought this subject before the House of Commons, and at an earlier period of the session Mr. Eastwick delivered an admirable speech on our relations with the Republics.

Boers did not hesitate to lay hands upon the particular districts which they coveted. In the year 1838 the Griqua territory was divided between the two chiefs Andries Waterboer and Adam Kok. The boundary-line was clearly defined by treaty, and no impartial person who has read the documents and studied the maps which have been published by the Cape government can for a moment doubt that the land which the Free State Boers now claim to have purchased from Adam Kok belongs to Nicholas, the son and successor of the late Andries Waterboer. It is not necessary to enlarge on this subject, because General Hay, the Acting Governor of the Cape Colony, has fully vindicated the native title to these lands, and has appointed, at the request of Waterboer, a British magistrate to preserve order at the diamond-fields. It is impossible to read the despatches which General Hay has addressed to Mr. Brand, the President of the Free State, without feeling that the interests of law, order, and morality have been effectually upheld by that gallant officer, and that he has taken one important step towards establishing in the interior a government which the whole world may respect, and which all good citizens should obey.

In my letter to Mr. Fowler, which was first published two years ago, I said that " it really seems as if events were now conspiring " to realize the dream of a South-African confederation." More than twelve years have elapsed since Governor Grey's despatch on this subject was written. In that document he displayed prophetic insight as well as practical statemanship. He vividly described the evils which resulted, and would continue to result, from the dismemberment of the empire in South Africa. As the only practical means of averting those evils he proposed the establishment of a Federal system of government, which should unite the British colonies, the two Dutch Republics, and the native territories under one central authority, while securing to each its own local government and institutions. He entered into many details to show the great advantages which all the members of such a confederacy would derive from their common union, and he more especially enlarged upon the value of that measure as a means of preventing internal wars, and of securing the permanent peace of the country. One passage will sufficiently explain his argument on this point—

The defects of the system thus described (*i. e.* the system which separates South Africa into rival states) appear to be, that the country must be always at war in some direction, as some one of the several states, in pursuit of its supposed interests, will be involved in difficulties, either with some European or native state. Every such war forces all the other states into a position of an armed neutrality or of interference. For if the state is successful in the war it is waging, a native race will be broken up, and none can tell what territories its dispersed hordes may fall upon; nor can the other states be assured that the coloured tribes generally will not sympathize in the war, and that a general rising may not take place. Ever since South Africa has been broken up in the manner above detailed, large portions of it have always been in a state of constant anxiety and apprehension from these causes."

The truth of these remarks will be borne out by every one who is acquainted with the history of South Africa during the period which has intervened since they were written. Take, for example, the case of the last Basuto war. To say nothing of the destruction of life, the injustice perpetrated on a native ally, or the alarm and demoralization created on our own frontier, the disturbance to peaceful colonization and industry which was occasioned by this war rendered it most injurious to the commercial interests of the Cape Colony. The climax of anarchy was reached when the Free State closed its courts, and Cape merchants, to whom the Boers owed hundreds of thousands of pounds, were unable to recover their debts by ordinary process of law. Of course the Free State, although containing all the natural resources which are necessary to the creation of a wealthy and prosperous state, suffered far more; and it is more than doubtful whether even "the fat lands of the Basutos" will compensate it for the heavy expenses, direct and indirect, entailed by the war. Since Sir George Grey wrote, the evils upon which he expatiated have grown more and more intolerable; and indeed a policy which secured the independence of small communities, whose only bond of cohesion was that supplied by a mutual contempt for the rights of the weaker races, could not fail to generate war and anarchy, and to prove most injurious to their own welfare, as well as to that of the Cape Colony and of Natal.

It cannot, I think, be doubted that the proposed Confederation would greatly lessen the danger of internecine war in South Africa. The discovery of gold and diamonds has again forced the subject upon the attention of the British Government. Fifteen thousand diggers, composed of very mixed elements, are now encamped on the banks of the Vaal River. They, like the inhabitants of the Orange Free State, cannot be released from their allegiance to the Crown without the authority of an Act of Parliament, and, taking all the circumstances into account, it is impossible that we can with honour shirk the responsibility of bringing them under the authority of a settled government. It is, however, impossible to deal adequately with this question except in connexion with the larger one of Confederation. It is therefore satisfactory to know that Sir Henry Barkley has assumed the governorship of the Cape Colony, with an earnest desire to establish a South African Dominion modelled upon that of Canada.

If I have appeared to write too hopefully of the future of a Federal system of government, it is not because I shut my eyes to the difficulties which must always attend the administration of affairs in a country inhabited by different races. Those difficulties will, in some shape or other, continue to exist so long as civilized nations practically reject the Christian doctrine of the essential brotherhood and equality of the human race. But the political union, on equal terms, of men, whether black or white, whether English or Dutch, would be a great step towards softening and, in time, destroying the hateful antipathies of race. Although in the present state of the world it is hopeless to look for the early dawn of the golden age, there is reason to believe that in South Africa, at least, the people are learning the truth of the classic apophthegm, that "nothing can be profitable "which is either dishonest or cruel." Let us, too, endeavour to learn the same lesson.

I am, my dear Sir,

Yours faithfully,

F. W. Chesson.

www.ingramcontent.com/pod-product-compliance
Lightning Source LLC
Chambersburg PA
CBHW021530090426
42739CB00007B/871

* 9 7 8 3 7 4 4 7 1 8 7 4 5 *